LANDS OF THE SOUTHERN CROSS

ENCYCLOPEDIA OF DISCOVERY AND EXPLORATION

Aldus Books London

10

LANDS OF THE SOUTHERN CROSS

BY JULIAN HOLLAND

Executive Coordinators: Beppie Harrison
                       John Mason

Design Director: Guenther Radtke

Editorial: Maureen Matheson
           Jill Gormley
           Marjorie Dickins

Picture Editor: Peter Cook

Research: Lynette Trotter

Cartography by Geographical Projects

Contents

Left: English emigrants to Australia watch the shore recede as they set off for the other side of the world.

Frontispiece: the Aborigines, the original inhabitants of Australia, naturally objected to the Europeans wandering over their territory. Here two British explorers face an attack by hostile Aborigines near the Victoria River in northwestern Australia in 1855.

List of Maps

The illuminated globe highlights in blue Australia and New Zealand, the exploration of which is the subject of this book. The globe also shows the islands of Indonesia and Malaysia stretching away to the north, and the continent of Antarctica in the south.

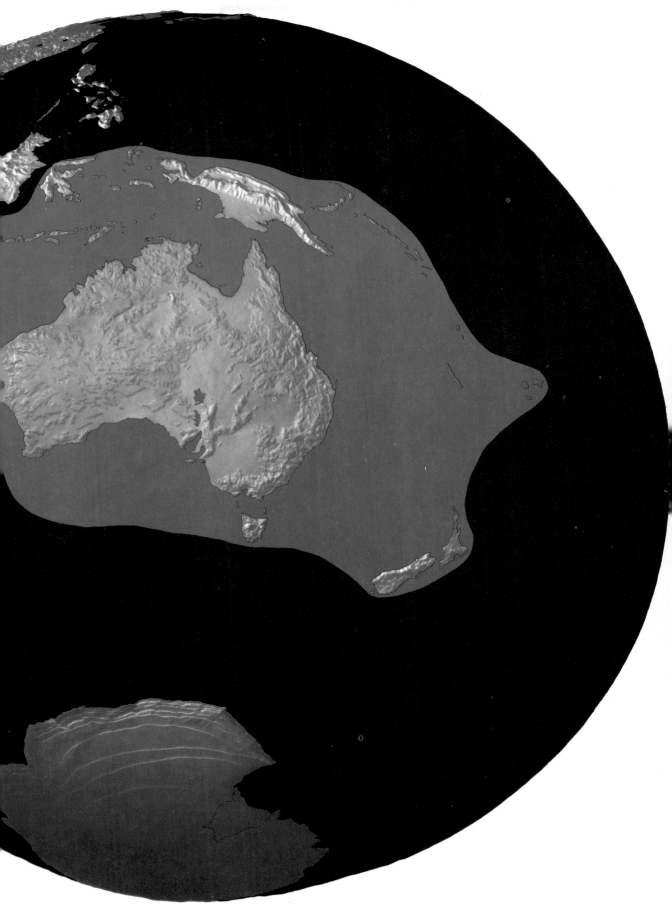

Below: to early explorers Australia
seemed a barren land unsuited to
trade or colonization. Even today some
areas reflect this view, like a movie
set showing the dawn of the world.

The Search for a Continent

1

The continent of Australia has always been one of the isolated parts of the world. The only continent to lie entirely within the Southern Hemisphere, Australia is surrounded on three sides by vast seas that for thousands of years remained uncharted. In prehistoric times the island groups situated immediately to the north of Australia served as stepping-stones for a few Stone Age men to move into the great southern land mass. But in later years these islands, with their erratic sea lanes and narrow winding channels, formed an effective barrier to the approach of large ocean-going ships from the other side of the world. Australia's isolation was complete. It is not surprising, then, that no men from the civilized world tried to settle on this island continent of nearly 3,000,000 square miles until the late 1700's.

The Aborigines, however, came to settle long before this. Walking overland, and paddling their boats over the sea from the Javanese islands to the north, they brought only their dog, the dingo, for company. This was 16,000 years or more ago, when Australia's great Lake Eyre was still the center of a lush landscape, where huge prehistoric animals roamed over the grassy plains and drank from the well-watered rivers. But when the rains ceased to fall—perhaps only 5,000 years ago—and the volcanoes discharged their last lava, Australia assumed its forbidding air of a ready-made location for a film about the dawn of the earth.

The Western world had always believed in the existence of an Australian continent. The Greeks insisted on a land mass in the south to balance the earth on its axis. One of the fragments left by the Greek historian Theopompus, writing in about 350 B.C., gives the story of a king who told of "certain islands named Europia, Asia, and Libia, which the Ocean Sea circumscribeth and compasseth round about and that without this world there is a continent or parcel of dry land which in greatness is infinite and immeasurable. And he told of its green meadows and pasture plots, its big and mighty beasts, its gigantic men who, in the same climate, exceed the stature of us twice, its many and divers cities, and its laws and ordinances clean contrary to ours."

The Greco-Roman world feared the other side of the equator. Yet, by the time of Ptolemy of Alexandria in A.D. 150, men had ventured far enough to the south and east for this early geographer to know in some detail about the Malay Peninsula. Ptolemy drew a

The Aborigines were Australia s first settlers. They lived as best they could off a land that was often barren and harsh. The coming of the white man changed the face of Australia and threatened the Aborigines' way of life but some of the isolated tribes still preserve the customs and life style of their ancestors.

map of the world. What he did not know, he theorized about. When he came to the limit of his knowledge about Asia he extended the land mass indefinitely to the east and south. When he came to the limit of his knowledge of Africa he extended the continent southward. And in the extreme south of the world, joining Asia and Africa, he created *Terra Incognita* (the unknown land).

For over a thousand years, while Christendom with its deep distrust of science held back all inquiry in western Europe ("How could men standing upside down be created in God's image?"), Ptolemy's *Terra Incognita* remained the limit of man's concept of Australia. Except, of course, for those who had already found it—the Aborigines.

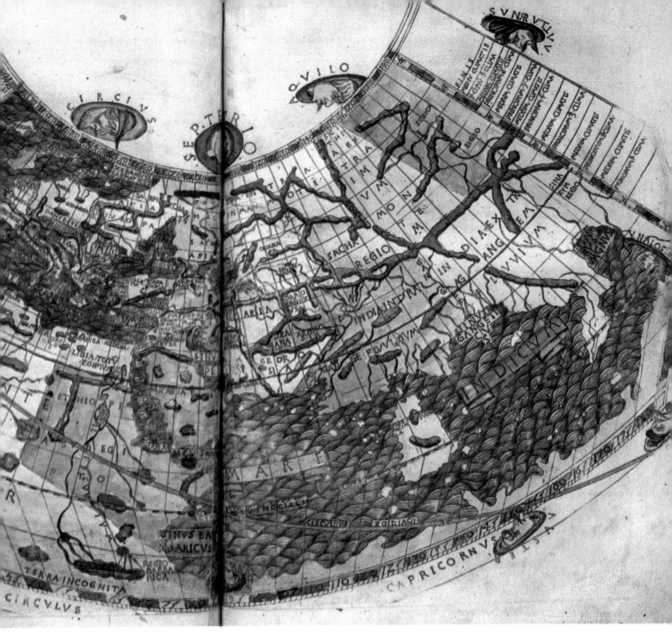

Traditionally, anthropologists divide mankind into three main groups: Caucasoid, Mongoloid, and Negroid. But the Australian Aboriginal is essentially different from these three types. The Aborigines are a dark-skinned people with slender hands and slight buttocks, low foreheads, deep-set eyes, and erect, hairy bodies.

All the main races of the world had a center from which they later dispersed. The starting point of the Australoid (as the Australian Aboriginal is often called) was Java and the other islands to the north of Australia. Some Australoids migrated to Malaya and India, but the main movement was south into the great southern continent.

Scientific dating methods indicate that the Aborigines came to Australia more than 16,000 years ago when the level of the sur-

Early mapmakers used to draw a vague Southern Continent in the South Pacific which they called *Terra Australis Incognita*, the unknown southern land. This map, based on a description by the Greek geographer, Ptolemy, who lived about A.D. 150, shows this imaginary continent stretching across the southern part of the globe.

11

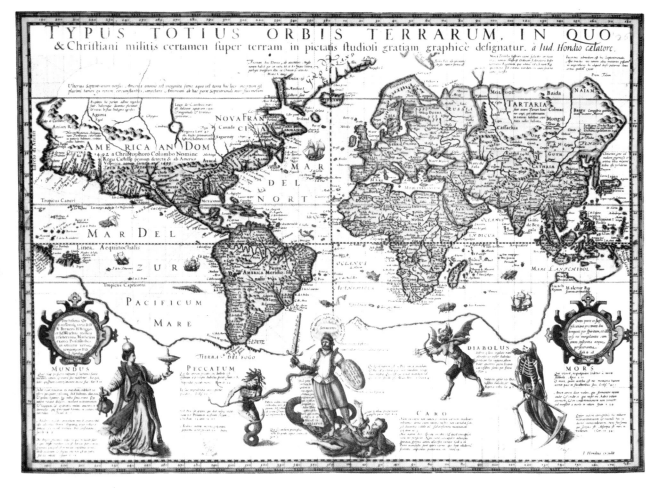

Above: as late as 1596, maps like this "Christian Knight map" still showed the imaginary Southern Continent, although by now two points, Tierra del Fuego and the tip of Australia, had been discovered.

rounding sea was at least 270 feet lower than it is today. The enormously wide Sahul Shelf joined New Guinea to Australia, enabling the migrating Australoids to walk the last stage of their journey into their new country. There was water to cross earlier however. The narrow straits east of Borneo and south and east of Timor have cut off New Guinea and Australia from Asia from prehistoric times. But the Australoids were good swimmers and some had small boats. It was not difficult for them to cross narrow stretches of water, interspersed as these were with innumerable islands.

The Australoid was a simple food-gatherer who moved only as he needed fresh hunting grounds. He did not till the land or grow crops, but lived on snakes and lizards, grubs and roots, fish, and the occasional kangaroo or crocodile. The Aborigines had no knowledge of metal or iron. They fashioned their weapons and tools from stone, bone, wood or shell. Their weapons, though simple, were often ingenious. With the woomerah (spear-thrower), they were able to hurl their spears great distances. The most famous Aboriginal weapon—the boomerang—could be thrown even farther than a spear. The boomerang is a flat, curved piece of hardwood which, when thrown skillfully, returns to the thrower if it misses its target. Aborigine men were skilled hunters who used their weapons with patience and accuracy.

A hardy people, the Aborigines could bear extremes of cold, heat, and humidity (the dampness in the atmosphere). In most regions they went naked. Mainly, tribes lived in the open, sometimes constructing makeshift shelters, but usually with only the sky for a roof. Their lack of material possessions increased their mobility and matched their nomadic way of life. For above all the Aborigines were wanderers, following the seasons and roaming across the Australian continent in search of food and water.

Long before the European discovery of Australia, the Aborigine had fully adapted himself to life on the southern continent and had developed a complex system of ritual and social custom. The Aboriginal life style was not easy for early visitors to comprehend. Most Europeans considered the Aborigines to be a lazy, stupid people without tradition or material wealth. William Dampier, the first Englishman to meet them, despised them utterly. "The

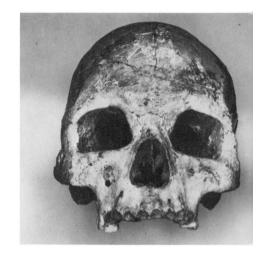

Above: skulls such as this link the Australian Aborigines with the natives of Java.
Below: an early drawing of Aborigines.

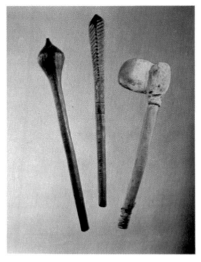

Above: Aboriginal weapons and tools were simple but often ingenious. This ax is simply a stone strapped to a sturdy stick. The other two weapons are just weighted sticks.
Left: the dingo, Australia's wild dog, is thought to have been brought to the continent by Aborigines.

inhabitants of this country are the miserablest people in the world. The Hodmadods of Monomatapa [presumably the Hottentots of Africa], though a nasty people, yet for wealth are gentlemen to these; who have no houses and skin garments, sheep, poultry, and fruits of the earth, ostrich eggs, etc., as the Hodmadods have; and setting aside their human shape, they differ but little from brutes."

Eighty years after Dampier's verdict, Captain James Cook visited Australia's eastern coast and gave a far more sympathetic appraisal of the Aboriginal way of life. "From what I have said of the natives of New Holland [as Australia was then known] they may appear to some to be the most wretched people upon earth; but in reality they are far more happier than we Europeans, being wholly unacquainted not only with the superfluous, but with the necessary conveniences so much sought after in Europe; they are happy in not knowing the use of them. They live in a tranquility which is not disturbed by the inequality of condition. The earth and sea of their own accord furnish them with all things necessary for life. They covet not magnificent houses, household-stuff, etc.; they live in a warm and fine climate, and enjoy very wholesome air, so that they have very little need of clothing; and this they seem to be fully sensible of, for many to whom we gave cloth, etc., left it carelessly upon the sea beach and in the woods, as a thing they had no manner of use for; in short they seem'd to set no value upon anything we gave them, nor would they ever part with anything of their own for any one article we could offer them. This in my opinion, argues that they think themselves provided with all the necessaries of life, and that they have no superfluities."

Unfortunately, Cook's judgment was not shared by many of his fellow Europeans. In 1788, when Sydney was founded, there were probably 300,000 Aborigines in Australia. Today there are fewer than 80,000. Deprived of their hunting grounds and with their traditional way of life threatened, exposed to new diseases brought by the Europeans, and even on occasion shot down by Australian colonists, the Aborigines swiftly lost their independence and with it their will to live. By the mid-1800's, many people believed the Aborigines were a dying race.

Below: map showing the main geographical features of Australia and New Zealand, and part of Indonesia. The important cities and the political frontiers are also shown.

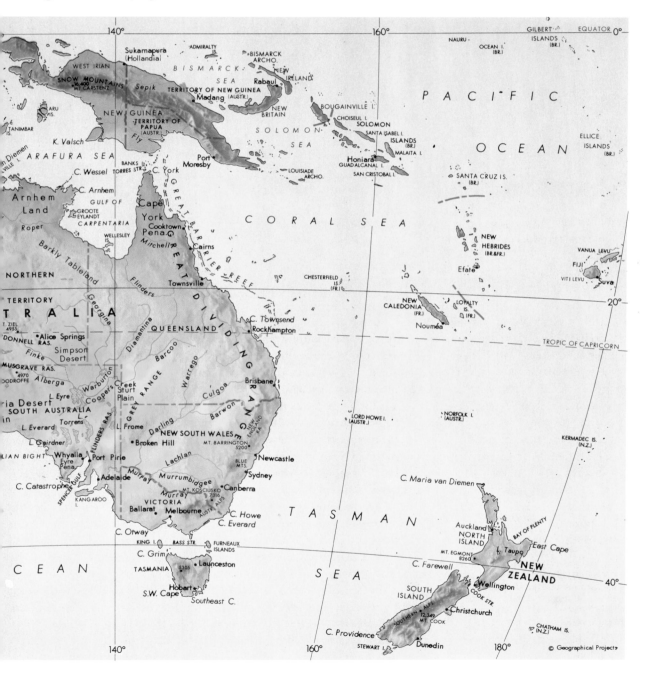

© Geographical Project

Above: when this coin dating from the reign of Ptolemy IV (ruler of Egypt, 221–203 B.C.) was found near Cairns, Queensland in 1909, it raised a completely new question. Could the ancient Egyptians or other contemporary Mediterranean explorers really have reached Australia ? Or had the coin simply been dropped by some more recent traveler ?

Above a creek near Cairns, Queensland, a coin of Ptolemy IV, the Egyptian king from 221–203 B.C. was found in 1909. Was it a keepsake dropped by a settler? Or were traders walking about northern Queensland 2,000 or more years ago? Embedded in a banyan tree near Darwin, Northern Territory, a soapstone figurine of a Taoist god was found in 1879. Taoism was the Chinese imperial religion during the A.D. 600's. Was the figurine carried to Australia by missionaries of the age? On Winchelsea Island, off the northwest coast of Groote Eylandt in the Gulf of Carpentaria, a piece of Ming china dating from the 1400's or 1500's was found in 1948. Again, how did it get there?

The question of who visited Australia in the centuries before European exploration began remains unanswered. But it is not unlikely that the Asian peoples—those for whom the China Sea and the Indian and Pacific oceans were daily trade routes—knew of the great southern continent and had touched on its shores.

The Malays of the islands must have been visiting the north coast of Australia for centuries. When Matthew Flinders was making the first circumnavigation of the continent (1801–1803) he came across six Malay proas (boats with large lateen sails) fishing in the Gulf of Carpentaria. The Javanese especially were an energetic, adventurous

Left: the Javanese have long been adventurous, resourceful fishermen. It is thought possible that they reached Australia in their fishing expeditions long before the continent was discovered by European explorers.

Below: various Chinese remains have been found in Australia and they raise the question of whether the Chinese were among the country's first explorers. They could have reached Australia on trading voyages in junks such as this.

people who had built a considerable empire in the East. Standing, as their country did, at the center of the ancient Oriental trade routes, the Javanese could not but have passed on their knowledge of Australia to the rest of the Asian commercial world. But the Chinese, the Hindus, and the Arabs were interested primarily in trade, and Australia offered little encouragement. Whoever came, they went away quickly, deterred by the hostility of the land and its people.

A map made in Italy in the 700's shows a southern segment added to the three continents (Europe, Africa, Asia) of the then known world. The legend explains: "Here lies a fourth part beyond the Interior [Indian] Ocean which on account of the heat of the sun is unknown to us where may live the fabulous antipodeans." Ptolemy's unknown land is to be seen on many European maps made during the next seven centuries. But the shape of its outline was just a crude guess unsupported by any scientific evidence.

Historians are uncertain about which Europeans discovered Australia and when, but it is possible that the Portuguese reached it between 1511 and 1529. Portuguese traders were predominant in the East Indies at this time. However, lack of documentation—its absence is easily understood—means it may never be possible to date the discovery precisely.

Below: probably the first Europeans to see the large mysterious "Southern Continent" were the Portuguese in small merchant ships like the one in the Holbein drawing below. During the late 1400's the world had been divided in two by the Pope, the west for Spain to explore and the east for Portugal. Because the new continent was in the Spanish half of the world, Portugal did not record the discovery.

Portugal discovered the Moluccas—the famed Spice Islands—in 1511, and established them as a colony two years later. But in 1516 Spain began to dispute the ownership of the Moluccas on the grounds that they were in her "half" of the world. (In 1493 Pope Alexander VI had settled a Line of Demarcation, dividing the world between Spain and Portugal for colonial exploitation. The following year the two countries agreed to move the dividing line farther west. This gave Portugal the right to explore territory that is now part of Brazil, but left the ownership of the Moluccas in doubt.)

The quarrel over the Moluccas came to a head in 1527 when the Spaniard Don Alvaro de Saavedra, while on a rescue expedition, landed there. Bargaining began, and in 1529 the Spanish emperor withdrew his claim to the islands on receipt of suitable compensation from Portugal.

The king of Portugal forbade upon pain of death the export of any marine chart which showed the route to Calicut, an Indian port on the Arabian Sea. Portugal feared that publication of any information about the lands in the southern seas might help and encourage other powers to rival her supremacy. Nor could they ever document or admit to any exploration in what was the agreed "Spanish half" of the world.

The evidence for the Portuguese discovery of Australia is essentially based on the Dieppe Maps, a series of maps produced in France, the earliest of which is dated 1541. The French were the world's best hydrographers (charters of seas, lakes, rivers, and other waters) and cartographers, but even by 1529 no Frenchman had been farther south than Sumatra. Yet here at last was a map actually showing part of Australia instead of the imaginary continent found on earlier maps. The Dieppe Maps were undoubtedly made from the combined observations of a number of people who had been to the lands they show. And the major clue to the Portuguese as the pioneer explorers lies in the considerable number of Portuguese place names to be found on the maps. Thus, *Terre Ennegade* plainly comes from *Tierra Anegada,* meaning "land under water" or "sunken shoal"; *Baie Bassa* is from *Bahia Bassa,* meaning "low bay"; *Anda ne barcha,* a part of the legend on the Dieppe Maps, is straight Portuguese.

Because of Portugal's unwillingness to come into the open about its knowledge of Australia, the search for what had now be-

come known as *Terra Australis Incognita* (unknown southern land) continued. The Flemish geographer and mapmaker Gerhardus Mercator made a map of the world in 1569. It showed a southern continent and the existence of a strait separating it from New Guinea. A Portuguese navigator, Pedro Fernandez de Quiros, argued at length for the existence of the Southern Continent. He had sailed into the South Pacific with the Spanish explorer Alvaro Mendaña in 1595, when they had discovered first the Marquesas Islands and then the Santa Cruz Islands farther west. Quiros was anxious to continue his exploration. In 1605, he was commissioned by the governor of Peru to go out to settle the Santa Cruz Islands, and then continue his search for the *Terra Australis Incognita*.

With two well-armed vessels and a pinnace, Quiros reached the New Hebrides Islands, about 1,000 miles east of Australia. Con-

The French produced superb maps in the 1500's although they were not themselves very adventurous sailors. Their maps were drawn from the combined observations of sailors and explorers of various nationalities. This map, drawn by Jean Rotz, is one of the Dieppe Maps. It shows a large continent in the south with several Portuguese place names, supporting the theory that the Portuguese had at some time visited Australia.

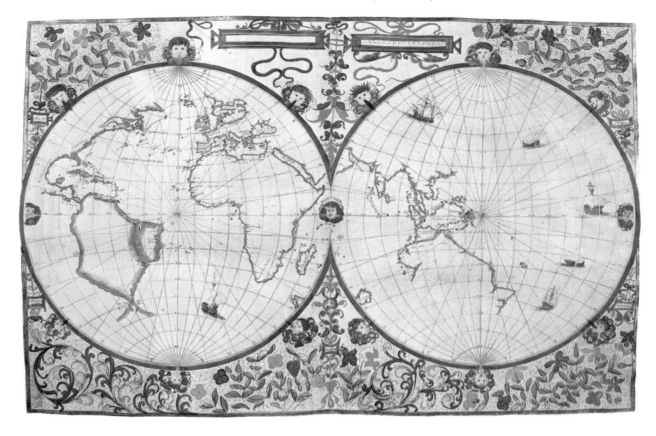

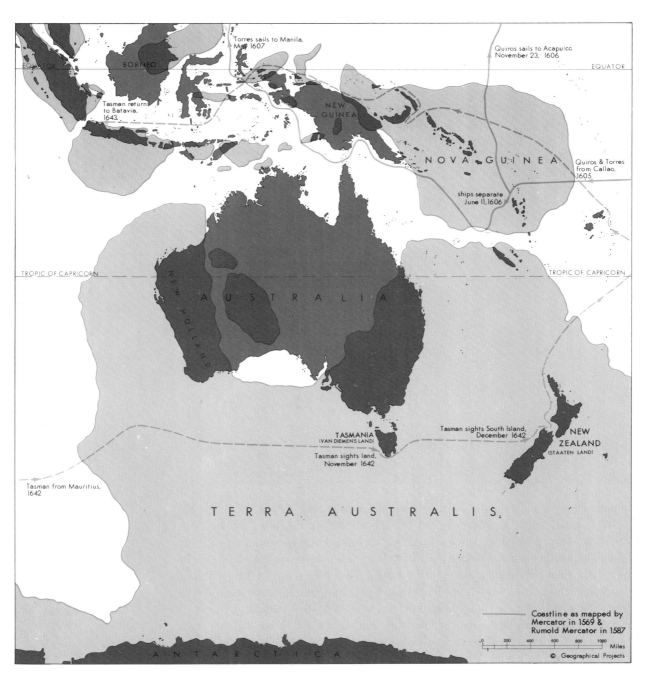

Torres sails to Manila, May 1607

Quiros sails to Acapulco November 23, 1606

EQUATOR

BORNEO

EQUATOR

Tasman returns to Batavia, 1643

NEW GUINEA

NOVA · GUINEA

Quiros & Torres from Callao, 1605

ships separate June 11, 1606

TROPIC OF CAPRICORN

TROPIC OF CAPRICORN

NEW HOLLAND

A U S T R A L I A

TASMANIA (VAN DIEMEN'S LAND)

Tasman sights South Island, December 1642

NEW ZEALAND (STAATEN LAND)

Tasman sights land, November 1642

Tasman from Mauritius, 1642

T E R R A   A U S T R A L I S.

Coastline as mapped by Mercator in 1569 & Rumold Mercator in 1587

0   200   400   600   800   1000
Miles
© Geographical Projects

A N T A R C T I C A

vinced that he had found the Southern Continent, he named the island Austrialia del Espiritu Santo, in honor of Spain's ally Austria. One night Quiros' ship, the *San Pedro y Paulo* disappeared suddenly and mysteriously. It is thought that the crew, wearied with the long and hazardous voyage, had mutinied and set sail back toward the Americas. The other two ships searched, but found no trace of the missing vessel. While searching, Luis Vaez de Torres, commander of the *Los Tres Reyes* (the three kings), soon discovered that Espiritu Santo was only an island. He determined to continue

Terra Australis Incognita, as mapped by the Mercators, was a vast continent including both Australia and Antarctica. This map shows the outline of the imaginary continent, covering Australia and New Zealand, and demonstrates how Tasman effectively disproved the theory by sailing through what was shown on the map to be a vast land mass.

Right: helped by the growing accuracy of European cartographers, especially Mercator (left) and Hondius, Dutch sea trade began to expand and their ships to venture farther afield.

Below: this map, drawn by Mercator in 1569, clearly shows a narrow strait between New Guinea and Australia. It was drawn about 40 years before Torres first sailed through the strait.

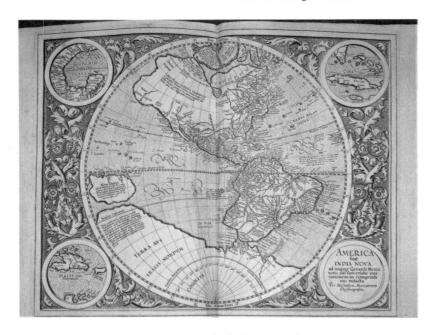

westward with his two ships to find the great Southern Continent.

In August, 1606, Torres touched the Louisiade Archipelago off the southeast tip of New Guinea. High winds forced him around the island's southern coast. He reached latitude 11° south—and here we have the first personal account of Australia. Torres wrote in his journal: "Here were very large islands and there appeared more to the southward. They were inhabited by black people, very stout and naked. Their arms were lances, arrows, and clubs of stone ill-fashioned." Torres' "very large islands" were the hills of Cape York, the northernmost tip of Australia.

It took Torres two months to sail through the strait now named after him. It was one of the finest feats of careful seamanship the world has known. He had found a much sought-after southern route from the Spice Islands into the Pacific. That no one was skilled or brave enough to follow him until Cook's voyage 164 years later makes Torres' feat even more remarkable. His, too, was Spain's last recorded venture in these parts. During the next hundred years, Australian exploration was to be almost wholly contained in the saga of Dutch commercial enterprise and in the wanderings of an English pirate.

GERARDUS MERCATOR NATUS
LUPELMUNDÆ I NON.MARTII ANNO
IↃIↃXII:VIXIT ANN.LXXXII.M.VIII.D.
XVI:DENATUS V NON.DECEMBRIS
ANNO CIↃIↃXCIV.

IUDOCUS HONDIUS NATUS IN
PAGO FLANDRIÆ DICTO WACKENE XVI
KALEND.NOVEMBRIS ANNO CIↃIↃLXIII:
VIXIT ANN.XLVII.M.VII.D.XXIX:DENAT:
US XIV KAL.MARTII ANNO CIↃIↃCXII.

Below: in the 1600's Dutch exploration reached its peak. The first Europeans to discover and map the Southern Continent officially, the Dutch called it New Holland and their maps showed elephants wandering in the interior.

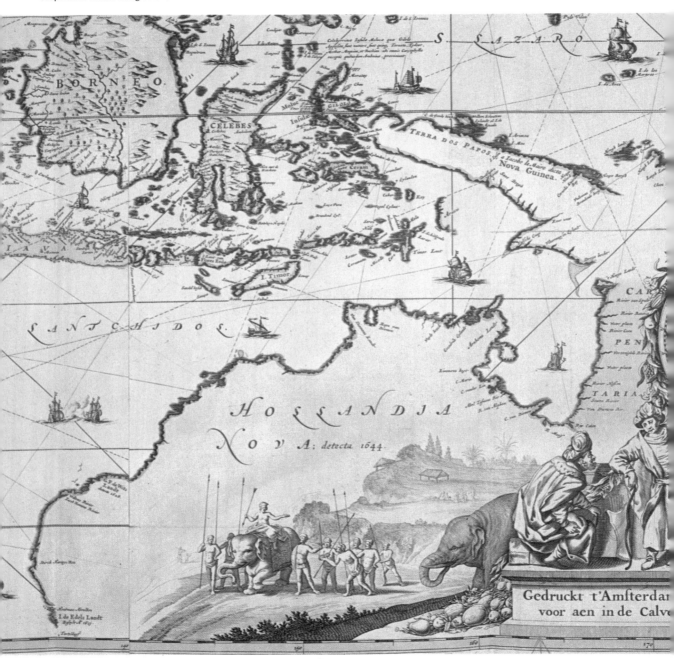

The Exploration of New Holland

2

The Dutch, unlike the Spanish, were not interested in saving souls. Nor were they solely interested in exploration. They were primarily interested in commerce. After liberation from Spanish oppression, the Dutch were determined to cripple Spain by robbing her of her ocean trade. In 1602, the Dutch East India Company was established. Four years later the pinnace *Duyfken* (little dove), under the command of Captain Willem Jansz, was sent to look for gold on the unexplored coast of New Guinea. Dutch explorers who came after Jansz were given this account of the historic voyage. "Captain Willem Jansz discovered the south and west coast of Nova Guinea [New Guinea] for about 800 miles from latitude 5° to 13¾° south. They found this extensive country for the greater part desert, but in some places inhabited by wild, cruel, black savages, by whom some of the crew were murdered. For this reason they could not learn anything of the land or waters, as had been desired of them; and by want of provision and other necessaries, they were obliged to leave the discovery unfinished. The farthest point of land was called in their map, Cape Keer-weer [turn again], situated at 13¾° south." Unknowingly, Jansz had crossed the Torres Strait and coasted south for 150 miles along the Australian shore thinking he was following the west coast of New Guinea. Jansz's voyage was the first recorded discovery of Australia.

In their frequent trips to the East, Dutch sailors soon learned to use the prevailing winds to best advantage. In 1611, Hendrik Brouwer, a Dutch captain, outward bound for Batavia (now Djakarta), then the capital of the Dutch East Indies, sailed due east from the Cape of Good Hope, before turning north toward the tropics. This route proved so successful that the Dutch East India Company ordered all later navigators to follow it. It was inevitable that sooner or later someone would overshoot the eastward leg of the journey and bump into the west coast of Australia.

Dirk Hartog, captain of the *Eendracht,* was the first to do so. He was racing east from the Cape when, on October 25, 1616, he ran onto an island, now named for him, off the west coast of Australia. Before leaving the island, Hartog nailed to a post a seaman's pewter plate which had been hammered flat. On the plate he scrawled the details of his visit: "A.D. 1616 on the 25th October there arrived here the ship the *Eendracht* of Amsterdam; skipper Dirk Hartog." Eighty-one years later, in 1697, Captain Vlamingh of the *Geelvink*

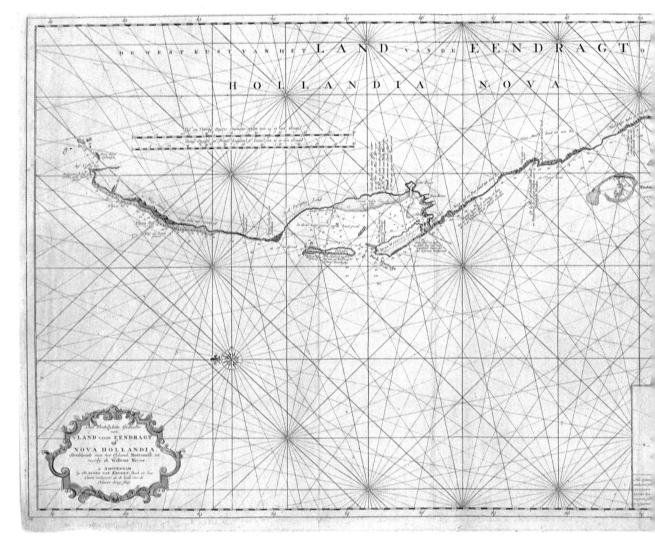

found Hartog's plate, replaced it with another, and brought the original back to Amsterdam. Another 104 years passed and Captain Hamelin of the French ship *Naturaliste,* found Vlamingh's plate, worn but still decipherable, lying in the sand.

During the next 10 years, Dutch ships traveled up and down the west coast of Australia, naming and charting their discoveries. In 1618, the *Mauritius* reached the Northwest Cape and the *Zeewulf* (sea wolf) touched on the coast near Port Hedland. In 1619, the vicinity of Perth was reached by the Dutchman Edel and the area was named after him—Edel's Land—on early Dutch maps. Houtman Abrolhos, the group of coral islands lying off the coast of Edel's Land, was also added to the map. Then, in 1622, the *Leeuwin* (lioness) sailed to the southwest corner of Australia and the cape was named after the ship.

In January, 1623, Jan Carstensz, in command of the two ships *Pera* and *Arnhem* was sent to look for gold and spices. The vessels were blown across the Gulf of Carpentaria to another new area which they called Arnhem Land. They found the Liverpool River and then turned north for Batavia. But somewhere in the Arafura

Sea, which lies between Australia and New Guinea, the two ships were separated. The *Arnhem* continued north, but the *Pera* turned east along the south coast of New Guinea. This time they followed the course of the *Duyfken,* past Cape Keer-weer, and south to Alligator Point before heading for home.

The south coast of Australia was discovered by the Dutch in 1627 when Captain Thyssen in the *Gulde Zeepaert* (golden seahorse) racing eastward, passed Cape Leeuwin and ran 1,000 miles along the shore. The land became known as Nuytsland after an important civilian on board, Pieter Nuyts, later to become ambassador to Japan and governor of Formosa. The *Gulde Zeepaert* became the first ship to cross the Great Australian Bight. But the irony of the journey was that Thyssen decided to turn back when he was within only a few miles of what is now the rich farm land of South Australia.

Dutch familiarity with Australia in only a quarter of a century of trading in the area was such that the land mass was soon called New Holland on the maps.

In 1629 the first Europeans were put ashore on the Australian mainland. The story begins with the shipwreck of the *Batavia,* headed for the Dutch East Indies. On the night of June 4, the ship was blown

Above: the Dutch discovery of the west coast of Australia happened purely by accident. A merchant ship, the *Eendracht* under its captain Dirk Hartog following the Cape route to the East Indies, ran onto an island off the Australian coast. This chart, published in 1750, shows that Hartog's landfall became known as Dirk Hartog Island, and the mainland as Eendragt (Eendracht) Land.

Right: the Dutch *fluit* or flyboat was a cheaply-built freighter which first appeared in shipyards in 1590. It was largely responsible for the realization of Dutch ambitions in Asia, Australia, and the South Seas.

Above: François Pelsaert, Dutch commander of the ship *Batavia* which in 1629 was shipwrecked off Australia's western coast while on a journey to the Dutch East Indies.
Left: one of the coral islands in the group known as Houtman Abrolhos, situated about 50 miles west of present-day Geraldton. It was on one of these small islands that the *Batavia* was shipwrecked.

onto the reefs of Houtman Abrolhos. François Pelsaert, the commander, ordered the cannon to be pitched overboard in the hope of floating the ship. But the *Batavia* was stuck fast, and as a heavy storm arose, they cut away the mainmast. At dawn, Pelsaert noticed an island nine miles away, with two smaller ones, no more than rocks, close to it. He ordered the women and children put ashore, while the crew struggled to salvage as much food as possible. In all, 180 people were landed on the large island and 40 on the smaller one. As the storm grew worse the *Batavia* broke up and 70 men perished.

On June 8, having found no fresh water on the islands, Pelsaert put to sea in a small boat on which had been built a covering deck with timbers from the wrecked *Batavia*. He hoped to find water on the mainland, about 25 miles away. The coast was rocky and barren with high cliffs. The small boat tried to put in at a sandy bay but surf and bad weather forced it to remain behind the breakers. They steered north in search of a safer landing. But always the cliffs and the breakers thwarted them. Five hundred miles from the wreck, and with barely enough fresh water for their own needs, Pelsaert decided the best course was to make for Java to enlist help.

Meanwhile, on the Houtman Abrolhos, Jerome Cornelis, the ship's under-merchant, had taken over. Soon after Pelsaert's departure, someone tasted water on the rocks which proved fit to drink and provided an inexhaustible supply. With the water problem solved, Cornelis seized control. He outlined his mutinous plan to the rest of the crew and executed 30 or 40 men who did not show enough enthusiasm for it. A few dissidents escaped to the smaller islands and rallied under a man named Weybehays. Eventually, Weybehays found himself with 45 men, all determined to defend themselves against Cornelis. Meanwhile, Cornelis raided the smaller of the islands killing everyone but seven children and five women. He and

Below: these three illustrations, all taken from Pelsaert's own account of the incident, show episodes in the story of the *Batavia* and her crew.
Top: the *Batavia* hits a coral island on the night of June 4, 1629.
Center: the ship breaks up and her crew put to sea in ship's boats to find refuge on nearby islands.
Bottom: Pelsaert himself sets sail (right) and makes his way between the islands in search of food, water, and help for his crew.

his men broke open the chests of merchandise rescued from the wreck and had clothes made for themselves from the rich material.

After declaring himself "captain general," Cornelis sent a party of 22 men to destroy Weybehay's force. When they were repulsed, Cornelis himself led a force of 37 men. They were met at the shore by Weybehay's men armed with spiked clubs. Again, the mutineers were routed. Finally Cornelis proposed a treaty of peace while trying to bribe some of Weybehays' company to betray their leader. But the men put more trust in Weybehays and informed him of Cornelis' offer. The next day, when Cornelis returned for an answer, they took him prisoner.

It was at this moment that Pelsaert returned to the scene in the ship *Saardam*. Seeing smoke on one of the islands he was overjoyed to find that some of his charges were still alive. A skiff was loaded with bread and wine, and Pelsaert rowed ashore. Weybehays met him at the water's edge and told him of the mutiny. There was still a large force of Cornelis' men on the main island and Pelsaert hastened

Above: While Pelsaert was away
seeking help, Jerome Cornelis, the
Batavia's under-merchant, seized
control. He and his fellow mutineers
executed 30 or 40 men who resisted,
broke open chests of merchandise, and
made clothes from the rich fabrics they
found. On his return, in the ship
Saardam, Pelsaert crushed the mutiny.
Only two mutineers were spared, and
marooned on the shores of Australia—
the first white 'settlers' on the vast
continent. They were never seen again.

Right: map of the western coast of
Australia, showing the landfalls by
explorers in the 1600's. It was on
this coast that the first European
settlers were put ashore by Pelsaert.

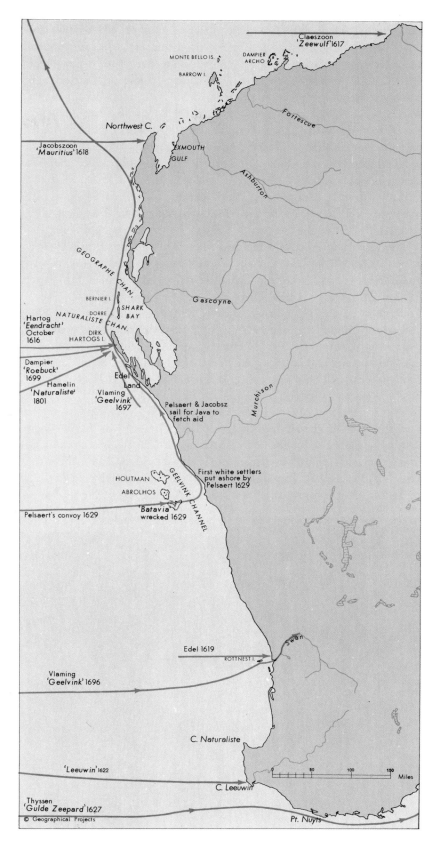

Claeszoon
'Zeewulf' 1617

MONTE BELLO IS.   DAMPIER
ARCHO.
BARROW I.

Fortescue

Northwest C.

Jacobszoon
'Mauritius' 1618
EXMOUTH
GULF

Ashburton

GEOGRAPHE CHAN.

Gascoyne

BERNIER I.
DORRE
NATURALISTE CHAN.   SHARK
BAY
Hartog
'Eendracht'   DIRK
October   HARTOGS I.
1616

Dampier
'Roebuck'
1699
Edel
Hamelin   Land
'Naturaliste'
1801   Vlaming
'Geelvink'
1697

Murchison

Pelsaert & Jacobsz
sail for Java to
fetch aid

First white settlers
put ashore by
Pelsaert 1629

HOUTMAN
ABROLHOS

GEELVINK CHANNEL

Pelsaert's convoy 1629   'Batavia'
wrecked 1629

Swan

Edel 1619
ROTTNEST I.

Vlaming
'Geelvink' 1696

C. Naturaliste

0   50   100   150
'Leeuwin' 1622   Miles

C. Leeuwin
Thyssen
'Gulde Zeepard' 1627
© Geographical Projects   Pt. Nuyts

back to the *Saardam*. He was just in time. A few minutes later, two boats came alongside manned by men wearing embroidered clothes and carrying weapons. Pelsaert demanded to know why they were armed, and threatened to sink them unless they threw away their weapons. Sensing defeat, they surrendered without a struggle and were quickly clapped in irons. The first man to be examined confessed to the murder of 27 men. That evening Weybehays brought his prisoner aboard, and the remaining brigands gave themselves up. Ten days later a council voted for the traitors' immediate trial and execution.

But two men escaped the death penalty. Their fate was to be marooned on the shores of the Australian continent, thus becoming Australia's first white "settlers." They were never seen again.

The Houtman Abrolhos claimed many Dutch ships in those early adventuring days. But for all their losses on the west coast of Australia, the long southern coastline remained a considerable lure to the Dutch East India Company. In August, 1642, the Dutch governor general Anthony van Diemen commissioned Abel Janszoon Tasman to make a thorough investigation of the seas to the south of Australia. Van Diemen's formal instructions were that: "All continents and islands which you shall discover, touch and set foot on, you will take possession of on behalf of their High Mightinesses the States General of the United Provinces."

The voyage had several important aims. The Dutch were eager to find the rich Solomon Islands, which had been "lost" since their original discovery by the Spanish in 1568. They were anxious to find a southern sea passage from the Spice Islands to Chile, where the Dutch had established a valuable trade with the Spanish colonies. At this time, Dutch ships sailed around the north coast of New Guinea

Above: the representative of Dutch commercial power in the 1600's was the Dutch East India Company, which sent out ships like these, superior to those of the rest of Europe.

Left: Abel Tasman (1603–1659) seen here with his wife and daughter. In 1642 he was commissioned by the Dutch governor general to explore the seas to the south of Australia (New Holland) and to take possession of "all continents and islands which you shall discover, touch and set foot on" in the name of The Netherlands.

before proceeding southeast across the Pacific. The Dutch East India Company hoped Tasman would find a shorter route somewhere to the south. The Dutch also wanted a more comprehensive exploration of the New Guinea coastline. And they were still not sure about the existence of the great Southern Continent. This last purpose was uppermost in Tasman's mind as the *Heemskerck* set sail from Mauritius with a larger ship the *Zeehaen* (sea-hen). His journal begins: "A voyage . . . for the discovery of the unknown Southland, in the year of our Lord, 1642."

Sailing rapidly before fair winds, Tasman sighted the rocky shore of what is now called Tasmania on the afternoon of November 24, 1642. He was just north of the Elliot Bay area—a hundred miles farther south and he would have missed land completely. He followed the coastline of Tasmania to the south and east, but often at too great a distance to make an adequate survey. On December 1, Tasman anchored off Cape Frederick Henry on the southeast coast in order to fulfill his first instruction—to claim the land for the Netherlands. But the seas were so rough and the surf so high, that the ship was unable to reach the shore. The carpenter swam ashore with the

Tasmanian Aborigines were simple people with no knowledge of domestic animals or agriculture. They wore few or no clothes and lived on sea food, wild vegetables, and small animals which they hunted. The coming of the white man brought war, a new diet, and disease, and in 1876 the last Tasmanian Aborigine, Truganini, died.

flagpole, planted it, and performed the colonizing ceremony himself.

Tasman called the island Van Diemen's Land in honor of the governor general. The discovery of Australia may always be in dispute, but there is no controversy over this island on its southeastern tip. In 1856, in recognition of its Dutch discoverer, the island's name was changed by the British colonists to Tasmania.

The *Heemskerck* and the *Zeehaen* spent two weeks looping the southern quarter of the island, and on December 4, Tasman determined to push eastward in search of the Solomon Islands. Nine days later, on December 13, 1642, they again sighted land. Presented with a coastline to starboard, Tasman was convinced he had found the

Southern Continent. Actually, he was looking at the western coast of New Zealand's South Island. A heavy southwesterly swell and the danger implicit in an unknown shore, prevented him from landing. For three days they sailed north until, rounding the northernmost cape of the South Island, they swung east into what is now called Golden Bay. That evening they dropped anchor in the protected harbor.

Although anxious to replenish his supply of fresh water, Tasman was wary of this unknown land and of its inhabitants. Would they prove friendly or hostile to the Dutch? Early the next morning the *Zeehaen*'s officers came aboard the *Heemskerck* for a counsel. It was decided that the island's inhabitants should be allowed to make the first move. Tasman counseled that no risk was to be taken. Their careful plans soon proved irrelevant, for as the officers were returning to the *Zeehaen,* they were attacked and overwhelmed by a boatload of Maori warriors. After killing four of the Dutch, the Maoris rowed rapidly toward shore. Tasman ordered the ship's guns to be fired, but the warriors escaped. The speed of the Maori canoes and the skill with which they were handled had surprised and impressed the Europeans. To avoid further trouble, Tasman ordered the ships to weigh anchor. As they sailed from the harbor, he named it Murderers' Bay.

The Dutch vessels continued north. But always the fierce Maoris and the rough surf prevented their landing. At last, Tasman was forced to abandon his hope of obtaining water and supplies from the hostile country. He charted a course for Batavia.

Although Tasman was the first European to sight New Zealand,

Right: Tasman's drawing of the events at Murderers' Bay shows: *A*, his own ships, the *Heemskerck* and *Zeehaen; B*, native canoes coming alongside the Dutch ships; *C*, a boat returning to the *Zeehaen* and being attacked by natives; *D*, a native canoe in detail; *E*, Dutch ships sailing out to sea; *F*, a pinnace towing the Dutch boat and casualties back to the ship.

neither he nor any member of his crew set foot on the land which they had discovered. They also missed the strait which separates New Zealand's two large islands. Thus, they sailed away convinced that they had been following the mainland coast of the unknown Southern Continent.

Tasman returned to Batavia via Tonga and the north coast of New Guinea. He had in fact circumnavigated Australia—although he never even sighted it—and thus proved that the newly discovered land of New Holland was not linked to any great continent farther to the south.

In a second voyage in 1644, Tasman was sent to explore the north and northwest shores of New Holland. His orders were to go beyond the farthest discoveries along the "west coast of New Guinea" (the Cape York Peninsula was still thought to be a southern extension of New Guinea, probably divided by a narrow strait from the Australian mainland) and then link up with the west coast of Australia. The Dutch were still anxious to find a channel separating Australia and New Guinea which would provide a shorter route to Chile.

Tasman failed to find the Torres Strait, but he did establish the

Below: when Tasman established the continuity of the coastline from Cape York to the Northwest Cape new maps had to be issued to sea captains and their navigators. During the 1600's maps were engraved on copperplate before being printed. So it was an easy task to smooth over the area to be revised and then engrave the new coastline. This map, published in 1680, is the revised version of Johann Janssen's earlier map showing the Australian coastline.

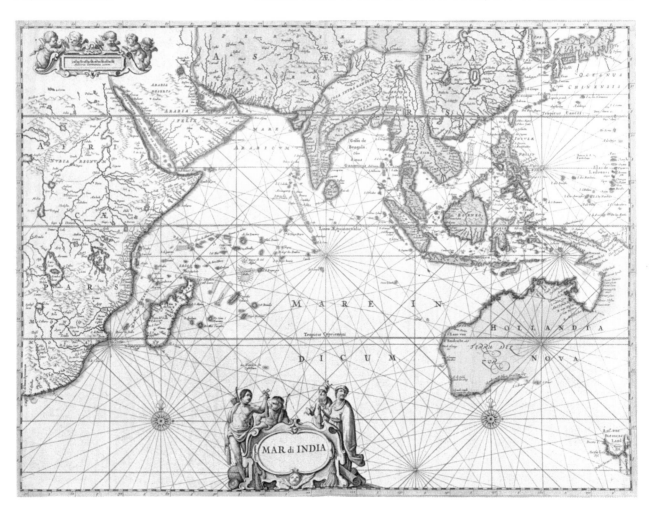

continuity of the coastline from Cape York to the Northwest Cape. He sailed around the Gulf of Carpentaria and named it after the company's Amsterdam president. On this voyage he followed the coastline more closely and made several observations on the land and its people. Of Anson Bay, south of Darwin, he wrote: "The coast is barren. The people are bad and wicked, shooting at the Dutch with arrows without provocation when they were coming on shore." Going round the Bonaparte Archipelago, he noted: "The people are savage and go naked. None can understand them."

The mapmakers had profited greatly from Tasman's voyage. They now knew with certainty that the three sides of the Australian continent—north, west, and south—were unbroken. They still believed, however, that there was a strait between New Guinea and Australia, even though their most skilled navigators had been unable to find it.

Above left: the *Mariner's Mirrour,* a book full of information for sailors, was translated from the Dutch into English and became standard equipment for every ship. The frontispiece shows various navigational instruments and sailors holding plumb lines.
Above right: a pirate, William Dampier, is the first Englishman known to have landed on the Australian coast.

A map entitled *Mar di India,* in the 1680 edition of Janssen's Atlas, shows the outline of Tasman's 1644 voyage but leaves the passage toward the Torres Strait open.

Like his first voyage, Tasman's 1644 expedition was a complete failure from a commercial point of view. He found no lands profitable for trade or exploitation. From this time on the Dutch began to lose interest in further exploration of the southwest Pacific and the Australian continent.

In 1688, the chance visit of an English pirate aroused a new—if short-lived—interest in the Australian continent. William Dampier was a self-trained naturalist who served as a navigator aboard the *Cygnet.* The pirate ship was jogging about the East Indies when a typhoon suddenly blew the ship south toward Australia's barren northern shore. "Being now clear of all the islands," wrote Dampier, "we stood off south, intending to touch at New Holland, a part of *Terra Australis Incognita,* to see what that country would afford us." They touched at New Holland on January 3, 1688, somewhere near Beagle Bay in what is now known as Dampier Land. The following day, after sailing 50 miles eastward into King Sound, they anchored in Cygnet Bay.

Here they remained for nine weeks despite the seamen's fears that Australia was populated by troglodytes—men whose heads grew under their shoulders and whose feet were so large that they served as sunshades when they lay down in the sun. Unlike all earlier visitors they did not just plant a flag or look for water, but lived ashore in one of the hottest regions of the world. The men slept in tents and hunted turtles and manatees (sea cows) for food while the ship's bottom was cleaned and her sails mended. During this time Dampier did more than any previous visitor to Australia to explore and observe the country and its inhabitants.

He returned to England in 1691, and in 1697 published his journal, *A New Voyage Around the World.* Dampier's tale astonished everyone. "New Holland," he wrote, "is a very large tract of land. It is not yet determined whether it is an island or a main continent, but I am certain it joins neither to Asia, Africa, nor America."

Dampier's journals awakened English interest in the Pacific and particularly in the great Southern Continent. Immediately after reading the journals, King William III ordered the Admiralty's first official voyage of discovery. Outfitted with a Royal Navy ship,

Dampier was sent back to the Pacific "to discover new countries and examine some of those already discovered." More particularly he was to strike the coast of New Holland, go to the north of New Guinea then explore to the east looking for *Terra Australis Incognita*. In effect his mission was the Tasman route in reverse, but he was given freedom to "steer any other course."

Dampier's original plan was to find the east coast that everyone had so far missed. He intended to approach New Holland from the east via Cape Horn. But there was a delay in fitting out his ship, and in order to avoid the turbulent Strait of Magellan during July and August, the Southern Hemisphere's winter months, he was forced to follow the traditional Cape of Good Hope route. To round the Cape

Above: off New Holland sailors often caught and ate sea cows or manatees. These whale-like mammals have peculiar mouths. Their upper lip is swollen and divided into two parts which can be moved separately. The two flippers or hands can be moved in all directions. The manatee is said to be the origin of legends about mermaids. Top: a woodcut dated 1547 of "fish called Manati."

of Good Hope, ships sailed southwest past the Cape Verde Islands almost to the coast of South America before turning southeast toward the Cape.

To add to his disappointment, Dampier was given only one ship instead of the two he had requested, and that unseaworthy craft was to sink before his return. The crew was poor, and the master, the man responsible for carrying out the captain's and navigator's orders, a heavy drinker. During their first night out, the *Roebuck*'s master nearly put the ship aground on the French coast. Most dangerous of all, Dampier's first lieutenant was a jealous professional sailor.

As ship's lieutenant, George Fisher was responsible for running the ship, and was outraged to find himself serving under an ex-buccaneer captain. There was trouble from the start. Dampier did not know how to command, and Fisher was open in his rebellion. They fought and insulted each other until Fisher went too far in publicly denigrating Dampier ("old dog, old villain, old, dissembling, cheating rogue") and Dampier went too far in striking Fisher with his cane and putting him in irons. Dampier put in at Bahia, Brazil, and consigned Fisher to the local jail before crossing the southern Atlantic and continuing around the Cape to Australia.

After a 7,000 mile uninterrupted voyage from Brazil, the *Roebuck* sighted land on July 31, 1699 at Dirk Hartog Island. Dampier sailed 900 miles around the western and northern coast of Australia to within a hundred miles of his previous landing at Cygnet Bay. As he turned the Northwest Cape, he looked back down Exmouth Gulf and wondered if he had not found the channel that separated New Holland from New Guinea. He determined to go back and explore as soon as he had found water. But water was something he was never to find in sufficient quantity.

After a brief landing at Shark Bay, Dampier went ashore at Roebuck Bay, just south of what is today the town of Broome, determined to capture an Aborigine who could lead them to fresh water. He laid a trap, offering a decoy to the Aborigines' hesitant threats. But the situation got so out of hand that Dampier was forced to fire his gun to frighten the inhabitants. At first he deliberately fired in the air. The lack of effect soon persuaded the Aborigines to ignore the noise. "Pooh, pooh, pooh!" they shouted, in imitation of the gun, and charged him. There was no alternative but to aim the

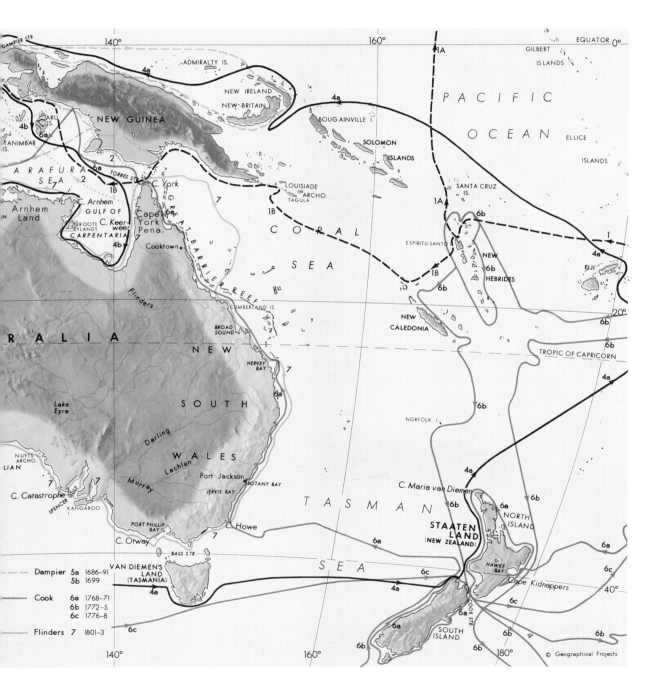

DAMPIER STR.

140° 160° EQUATOR 0°

1A GILBERT ISLANDS

PACIFIC

ADMIRALTY IS. 4a

NEW IRELAND 4a

NEW·BRITAIN BOUGAINVILLE I. OCEAN ELLICE

NEW GUINEA

4b ARU IS. 6a SOLOMON ISLANDS ISLANDS

TANIMBAR IS.

ARAFURA 4a 2 SANTA CRUZ IS.

SEA 2 TORRES STR. 1A 6b

7A 1B C. York LOUISIADE ARCHO. 1

C. Arnhem Cape TAGULA 1B E SPIRITU SANTO 4a

Arnhem Land GULF OF York CORAL NEW 6b FIJI

GROOTE EYLANDT C. Keer-weer Pena. 1B 6b HEBRIDES

CARPENTARIA 4b SEA 6b

Cooktown NEW 6b

RALIA Flinders CALEDONIA 20°

NEW CUMBERLAND IS. TROPIC OF CAPRICORN 6b

BROAD SOUND 7 6b

SOUTH 4a

Lake Eyre HERVEY BAY 7 NORFOLK I. 4a

WALES 6a 6b 4a

Darling Lachlan

NUYTS ARCHO. Murray C. Maria van Diemen 6b NORTH 6b

LIAN Port Jackson 6a ISLAND 6a

C. Catastrophe 7 7 JERVIS BAY BOTANY BAY TASMAN STAATEN 6b

SPENCER GULF KANGAROO I. LAND HAWKE 6a

PORT PHILLIP BAY C. Howe 7 (NEW ZEALAND) BAY 6a 6c

C. Otway SEA 6c Cape Kidnappers 40°

BASS STR. 6c

VAN DIEMEN'S 4a 4a 6a

Dampier 5a 1686-91 LAND COOK STR. 6a

5b 1699 (TASMANIA) 6c

SOUTH 6b

Cook 6a 1768-71 6a ISLAND 6b

6b 1772-5

6c 1776-8 6b 180°

Flinders 7 1801-3 6c © Geographical Projects

140° 160°

A
VOYAGE
TO
New Holland, &c.
In the Year, 1699.

Wherein are described,

The *Canary*-Islands, the Isles of *Mayo* and St. *Jago*. The Bay of *All Saints*, with the Forts and Town of *Bahia* in *Brasil*. Cape *Salvadore*. The Winds on the *Brasilian* Coast. *Abrohlo*-Shoals. A Table of all the *Variations* observ'd in this Voyage. Occurrences near the Cape of *Good Hope*. The Course to *New Holland*. *Shark's Bay*. The Isles and Coast, &c. of *New Holland*.

Their Inhabitants, Manners, Customs, Trade, &c. Their Harbours, Soil, Beasts, Birds, Fish, &c. Trees, Plants, Fruits, &c.

Illustrated with several Maps and Draughts; also divers Birds, Fishes, and Plants, not found in this part of the World, Curiously Ingraven on Copper-Plates.

By Captain *William Dampier*.

LONDON:
Printed for *James Knapton*, at the Crown in St. Paul's Church-yard, 1703.

Above: on returning to England, William Dampier published his journal of his adventures in New Holland. The journal made such an impression on King William III that he told the Admiralty to organize and finance their first official voyage of discovery, led by Dampier, the former pirate.

gun at one of them and wound him in an attempt to stop the attack.

With the scarcity of drinking water and little or no nourishing food, Dampier's men soon fell ill with scurvy. Scurvy was a dreaded disease among ships' crews. Caused by a lack of vitamin C, the illness was common, and often proved fatal among sailors who went for long periods of time without fresh fruit or vegetables. The *Roebuck* was forced to head north for the tropic islands. Dampier sailed around the north coast of New Guinea, rounded New Britain, then sailed back through the Dampier Strait on to the north coast of New Guinea again. Had he turned south he could not have failed to find the fertile eastern coast of Australia. But Dampier's problems were increasing. His journal notes: "The many difficulties I at this time met with, the want of convenience to clean my ship, the fewness of my men, their desire to hasten home, and the danger of continuing in these circumstances in seas where the shoals and coasts were utterly unknown and must be searched out with much caution and length of time, hindered me from prosecuting any farther at present my intended search."

Dampier set sail for England. A sick man, he brought the rotting *Roebuck* as far as the Atlantic. When the ship sprang a leak, the planks crumbled like biscuit around any repair. At last it went down off Ascension Island. Dampier was picked up a month later and reached England in August, 1701. He was immediately faced with a court martial. Fisher had escaped from the Brazilian jail and made his way back to England. He served such complaints to his sympathetic fellow officers that Dampier was found guilty, fined of his pay, and declared unfit ever again to command one of his Majesty's vessels. Nevertheless, two years later he was brought before Queen Anne and honored for his difficult voyage. His second book, *Voyage to New Holland,* was published in 1709. As in his earlier journal, Dampier recounted exciting adventures but condemned Australia as the most barren spot on earth.

Dampier's opinion was confirmed about the same time by two Dutchmen, Willem de Vlamingh and Martin van Delft. In 1696, Vlamingh was ordered to look for a Dutch ship thought to have been wrecked on the southern coast of Australia. Vlamingh never found the missing ship or any survivors. However, during his search he discovered Rottnest Island and ventured 20 miles up the Swan River where he caught two black swans. There he found the plate

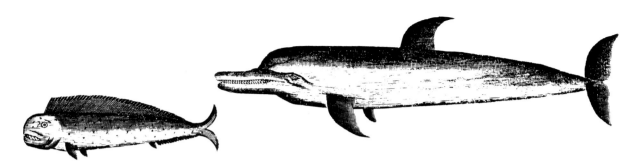

that Hartog had pinned to a post 81 years earlier. Only once in two months of coasting and exploring did he see any Aborigines. There was little compensation for the daily torment of the flies, the hopelessness of the sterile, sandy earth, and the inhospitable nature of the inhabitants.

In 1705, Martin van Delft was dispatched from Timor with three ships, the *Vossenbosch,* the *Wayer,* and the *Nova Hollandia,* "to explore the north coast of New Holland better than it had before been done." Delft sailed along the coast of Arnhem Land forming a poorer impression of the land and its inhabitants than even Dampier had done.

No one was any longer interested in Australia. Dutch commercial disappointment with the country, and Dampier's bleak picture of the land and its inhabitants, succeeded in putting off further major exploration for almost a century.

Above: Dampier filled his books with drawings of the fish, flowers, and birds he saw. The dolphin (right) was seen on the voyage and was considered a good omen by his sailors. The fish on the left is a dorado.

Below: explorers such as Vlamingh used rivers, like the Swan River on which black swans were caught, as highways into the interior of the new continent. But the inland areas seemed to the early pioneers to have no more commercial value than had the coast.

The Voyage of Captain Cook

3

Half a century elapsed. Only the east coast of Australia remained an inviting mystery. A Frenchman, Louis Antoine de Bougainville, came close to discovering it in 1768. De Bougainville sailed his frigate, *La Boudeuse* (the sulky woman), westward from the New Hebrides until he saw breakers stretching without end to the horizon. He was facing the Great Barrier Reef, and was within a few miles of the coast of Queensland. But the labyrinth of reefs and shallows, the milky frothing of the water around him, and the thunder of the flung-up water scouring the polyps (coral, sea anemones, jellyfishes) frightened him and he turned to the northeast for New Guinea. It was now Britain's turn again.

The British and the French were both seeking new colonial territories. In spite of the great discoveries made during the first voyages of exploration, many questions about the Pacific remained unanswered. The coast of New Holland had not yet been charted, and no one knew just how big the continent was. Tasman's New Zealand too remained a mystery. There was even room in the unknown for a huge continent other than New Holland.

In 1768, the British Royal Society requested that a ship be sent to the Pacific to observe the transit of Venus, an astronomical event due to occur in 1769. The Society had calculated beforehand that Tahiti would be the best vantage point for observing this phenomenon. The British Admiralty immediately seized the opportunity as a convenient cover for a thorough search for *Terra*

Left: this painting by William Hodges, depicts Cook encountering a waterspout off the coast of New Zealand. A waterspout is a tornado at sea, a whirling column of air and water that can cause serious damage even to large ships.

Right: Alexander Dalrymple, Fellow of the Royal Society. Although theories of a large southern land mass had been proved wrong with the discovery of Australia, he still believed one was needed to counterbalance the land north of the equator.

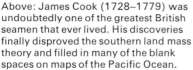

Above: James Cook (1728–1779) was undoubtedly one of the greatest British seamen that ever lived. His discoveries finally disproved the southern land mass theory and filled in many of the blank spaces on maps of the Pacific Ocean.

Above right: Cook chose a collier built in his home port of Whitby for his first Pacific voyage. The *Endeavour* was about 98 feet in length and just over 29 feet at her greatest width.

Australis Incognita. Alexander Dalrymple, a Fellow of the Royal Society, and a self-ordained British authority on *Terra Australis Incognita,* knew the Admiralty's purpose. Dalrymple had some very curious ideas about Australia. It was, he maintained, a continent containing some 50 million souls situated between New Zealand and Easter Island longitudinally and between the Solomons and Antarctica latitudinally. He went back to the ancient Greeks for his authority when he wrote: "a continent is wanting on the south of the equator to counterpoise the land on the north and to maintain the equilibrium necessary for the earth's motion." New Holland never entered into his reckoning, although in his book, *An Account of the Discoveries made in the South Pacific Ocean previous to 1764,* he re-

produces a map of New Holland similar to Tasman's map and mentions the existence of the Torres Strait.

Dalrymple assumed that he would be given command of the Admiralty ship detailed for the Pacific voyage. But there was a new pride in the Navy at this time—a professionalism instilled by the reforming zeal of Lord Anson. No amateur outsider was going to have charge of a British naval vessel. The Admiralty preferred instead to give command to a noncommissioned officer, a highly promising product of the lower deck. That man was James Cook.

Cook was born in 1728, at Marton, near Whitby in Yorkshire. His father was a farm laborer from Scotland. Cook's family was poor and as a youth he had little chance for a formal education.

At 18 he was apprenticed to John Walker, a Whitby shipowner. Walker lodged the boy in his own house when he was ashore and encouraged him to study. When he was only 25, Walker offered him command of a collier (a vessel for transporting coal). Surprisingly, Cook turned down the offer, choosing instead to join the Navy as an ordinary seaman. He served under Captain Hugh Palliser, an influential man who was later to become a Lord of the Admiralty. Palliser quickly recognized Cook's merit, and continued to encourage and support him for the rest of his naval career.

Cook was in no way unacceptable to the Royal Society, the original prompter of the expedition. In 1766, he had written a detailed description of an eclipse of the sun in Newfoundland which the Society had published and which had brought the self-taught sailor to the notice of men of science. He was introduced to the Society in 1768 and immediately accepted as one of its two official observers on the voyage. The second observer was an astronomer

Right: the *Endeavour* started life as the *Earl of Pembroke* carrying coals from England to Scandinavia, and Cook had her refitted before he sailed in her. A layer of thin oak boards was attached to her under-planking to protect her from shipworm; almost the whole rig was replaced; new cabins were built for officers; and she was armed with 10 guns on carriages and 12 swivel guns.

Above: Sir Joseph Banks sailed on Cook's first voyage to Australia. He has been called the "father of Australia" as he finally persuaded the British government to establish Botany Bay as a convict settlement. A botanist, he was President of the Royal Society for more than 40 years.

from the Greenwich Observatory in London, named Charles Green.

The expedition also included a wealthy young man from Lincolnshire, Joseph Banks, who brought with him two naturalists, two artists, and four servants. Like Cook he was ambitious and dedicated.

Cook, who still remained uncommissioned, was promoted lieutenant and given official command of the expedition at the end of May, 1768. He chose his own ship which was christened the *Endeavour*. It was a collier—an ugly, graceless, shallow-bottomed ship from Whitby. On August 26, 1768, the *Endeavour* sailed from Plymouth Harbour. Eight months later it reached Tahiti and the transit of Venus was duly observed on June 3. Cook then set sail again, his "additional secret orders" from the Admiralty instructing him: ". . . whereas there is reason to believe that a continent or land of great extent may be found . . . you are to proceed southward in order to make discovery of the land above-mentioned, or fall in with the land discovered by Tasman now called New Zealand. . . . You are also with the consent of the natives to take possession of convenient situations in the country in the name of the King of Great Britain."

As instructed Cook took the *Endeavour* south to the forties, an area between 40° and 50° latitude, as far as was practicable in July and August (midwinter in the Southern Hemisphere), and then swung into a zigzag course, northwest then southwest. Since rounding the Horn eight months earlier, Cook had sailed over much of the Pacific —through a lot of Dalrymple's *Terra Australis Incognita*. Then, on October, 6, 1769, the *Endeavour* touched on the east coast of New Zealand's North Island—the first European ship to sight the land since Tasman's voyage more than a century earlier. Banks and the ship's officers were convinced they had found the great Southern Continent. Cook, who doubted the existence of such a land mass, determined to establish the truth by a careful and thorough circumnavigation of the land. But first the ship's supply of water had to be replenished and the *Endeavour* dropped anchor in a protected bay.

For two days the men remained on board while Cook observed the coast from a distance. He was anxious to establish friendly relations with the inhabitants, but knew that Tasman had been prevented from landing because of the Maoris' hostility. Finally, on October 9, a small party ventured ashore. It turned back, however, when the inhabitants threatened to attack. A second attempt to land was

thwarted on the following day. Early on the third morning, Cook and his men set out again. While rowing toward the shore, Cook spied a Maori canoe and hurried to overtake it. Tupia, a Tahitian priest who had earlier come aboard to act as interpreter, called out to the occupants ordering them to halt. Instead the Maoris increased their speed toward the protection of shore. Hoping to frighten them into stopping, several shots were fired at the fleeing canoe. But the plan misfired. Suddenly, the Maoris turned and angrily attacked the sailors. Cook had underestimated the courage of the Maori warriors, who, with no comparable weapons, were determined to drive away the strangers. The sailors were forced to take aim, and in the ensuing struggle, three or four of the Maori men were killed. Cook was distressed at the turn of events.

"I am aware that most humane men who have not experienced things of this nature will censure my conduct in firing upon the people in their boat. Nor do I think myself that the reason I had for seizing upon her will at all justify me; and had I thought that they would make the least resistance, I would not have come near them; but as they did, I was not to stand still and suffer either myself or those that were with me to be knocked on the head."

His action had further unhappy consequences. The next day more than 200 angry Maori tribesmen gathered on the beach to prevent another attempt at landing. After naming the place Poverty Bay, "because it afforded no one thing that we wanted," Cook reluctantly set sail for the south. In a few days he was within the great sweep of

Above: explorers visiting the islands of New Zealand were greeted by Maoris in canoes. Cook described the craft as being long and narrow, and shaped very much like a New England whaleboat. The large canoes, built for war, carried from 40 to 100 men and were ornamented with an oddly designed figure of a man with a large tongue sticking out of his mouth. (Sticking out the tongue was one of the native signs of aggression.)

Above: Cook found much in the Maoris that he admired, but one of their customs horrified him. He wrote: ". . . and to show us that they eat human flesh, they bit and Naw'd the bone and draw'd it through their Mouths, and this in such a manner as plainly Shew'd that flesh to them was a Dainty Bit."

Hawke Bay. Here the inhabitants seemed eager to barter. But their friendship was short-lived. A canoe filled with armed Maoris approached the *Endeavour*. They had nothing with which to barter. Cook records the day's event in his journal:

"One man in this boat had on him a black skin, something like a bear skin, which I was desirous of having, that I might be a better judge of what sort of an animal the first owner had been. I offered him for it a piece of red cloth, which he seemed to jump at by immediately putting off the skin in his possession, and after that not at all, but put off the boat and went away, and with them all the rest. And the . . . boy, Tayeto, Tupia's servant, being over the side, they seized hold of him, pulled him into the boat and endeavoured to carry him off."

Quickly the sailors fired at the fleeing boat, and in the confusion Tayeto was able to jump overboard. Here, too, several Maori warriors were killed and for the second time Cook set sail without having secured water or supplies. He named the spot Cape Kidnappers to commemorate the incident. He then sailed the *Endeavour* some 70 miles farther south along the coast before turning around and sailing north again past Poverty Bay.

Cook was beginning to doubt whether he would find a favorable reception anywhere on the New Zealand coast, but as the *Endeavour* continued north the Maoris became more hospitable. He was able to replenish his supplies and observe the land and its inhabitants more closely. He noted a remarkable similarity between this warlike people and the inhabitants of Tahiti. Cook could not have known that the Maoris had come to New Zealand hundreds of years before from the Polynesian Islands he had just visited. But he comments several times on customs and traditions which existed in both lands. The Maori language was essentially the same as that of the Polynesians he knew. Tupia was immediately understood by the Maoris. The women had the same custom of cutting their bodies with shells to mourn their dead warriors. In the northernmost part of New Zealand, near Cape Maria van Diemen, Cook noted that the inhabitants possessed the cloth plant which he had admired so greatly in Tahiti. The climate of New Zealand was not favorable to the tropical plant's growth and the Maoris had learned to cultivate New Zealand's native flax for everyday clothing use. Nevertheless, the Tahitian plant was carefully preserved by the Maoris because tradition said that it

Below: the Maoris were warlike people. They greeted the white explorers in war canoes while armed warriors in fortified villages on the cliff tops waited and watched, ready to attack.

had been brought to the country by ancestors of the inhabitants.

One custom, however, distinguished the Maori people in the European eyes and filled Cook and his crew with horror. Several times, while rounding the North Island, they had heard rumors and seen evidence of cannibalism. But it was not until the *Endeavour* anchored in Tasman Bay on the South Island that their suspicions were confirmed. Cook's journal describes the discovery: "Soon after we landed, we met with two or three of the natives who not long before must have been regaling themselves upon human flesh for I got from one of them the bone of the forearm of a man or woman, which was quite fresh and the flesh had but lately been picked off, which they told us they had eat. They gave us to understand that but a few days before they had taken, killed, and eat a boat's crew of their enemies or strangers . . . they look upon all strangers as enemies."

Despite the horror which Cook felt about this savage custom, he greatly admired the Maori people. At the Bay of Islands he visited a *pa*—the Maori name for a fortified village—and commented on the expert construction, "especially considering the tools they had to work with, which are made of wood and stone." As a life-long seaman, he carefully noted every detail of their craft and pronounced their boats excellent. Cook respected the Maoris' pugnacity and courage. Before leaving New Zealand he concluded: "All their action and behaviour toward us tended to prove that they are a brave, open, warlike people and void of treachery."

He was no less impressed with the land of New Zealand than with its inhabitants. He noted that all European greens and plants would grow there. So great was his admiration that he returned to New

Above: in a Maori *pa* or village each family had its own cluster of houses, one for sleeping, one for food storage, and one for cooking. Meeting houses with carvings and decorations were built by men as symbols of importance.

Below: Queen Charlotte Sound was a favorite anchorage for Cook. He said, "it is a collection of some of the finest harbours in the world."

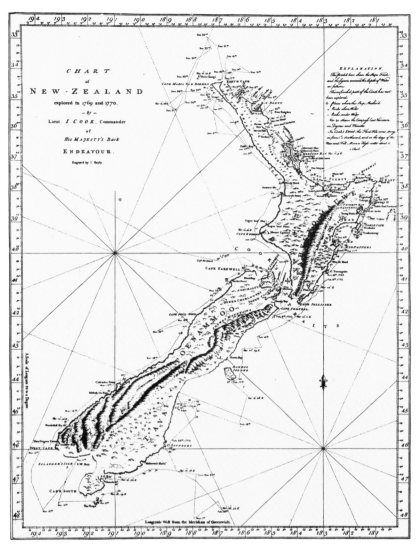

CHART
of
NEW·ZEALAND
explored in 1769 and 1770.
- by -
Lieut: I. C O O K, Commander
of
His MAJESTY'S Bark
ENDEAVOUR.

Cook was not only a great sailor but a careful and accurate cartographer. In this detailed chart of New Zealand he appears to have made only a few errors. Most important was his recognition that New Zealand was not part of a large Southern Continent, but two islands separated by a strait.

Zealand on each voyage he made to the Pacific—using Queen Charlotte Sound as a base and rendezvous.

The *Endeavour* completed its 2,500-mile close-in navigation of New Zealand in less than six months. Cook had established that the land first discovered by Tasman was not the legendary Southern Continent, but two large islands separated by a narrow strait (Cook Strait). He surveyed and charted as he went, and in this part of the voyage alone established himself as one of the greatest sailors of all time.

Cook sailed from New Zealand on March 31, 1770. Three weeks later he was headed for what is now the Bass Strait, when uncertainty and a southwesterly gale caused him to "bring to." When day broke on the morning of April 19, Lieutenant Hicks, on duty, sighted the southeast corner of Australia. Cook named it Point Hicks, after the young lookout. They turned northeast along the coast, but Cook had already seen enough of the seas and the winds to

guess that Van Diemen's Land was separated from the mainland by a sizable channel.

Cook sailed up the coast surveying as he went and looking for a safe harbor. After missing Jervis Bay, which could easily have sheltered the entire British Fleet, the *Endeavour* sailed into Botany Bay on April 29. It was a historic moment.

They remained at Botany Bay for nine days and Banks and his fellow naturalists filled Cook's cabin with innumerable plants and other specimens. While the naturalists collected their samples, the party took on wood and water and observed the strange surroundings. They saw kangaroo dung, trees with steps cut into their sides, canoes which were more primitive than any they had ever come across, and huts made from the bark of trees. On landing, they raised the flag and, with an inscription cut in a gum tree, claimed the land for England.

Unlike the Maoris, who had steadfastly protected their shores, the Aborigines, after an initial attempt to stop Cook landing, avoided all contact with the English sailors. Often when surprised in the middle of cooking their meals, they would flee into the bush. "The natives do not appear to be numerous," wrote Cook, "neither do they seem to live in large bodies but dispersed in small parties along by the water side. Those I saw were about as tall as Europeans, of a very dark colour but not black nor had they woolly, frizzled hair but black and lank like ours. No sort of clothing or ornaments were ever seen by any of us upon any of them or in or about any of their huts, from which I conclude that they never wear any. Some that we saw had their faces and bodies painted with a sort of white paint or pigment."

Cook was cool and factual, an admirable chronicler. It was only when he came to a description of the country itself that he was misleading. "We made an excursion into the country," he wrote on May 1, "which we found diversified with woods, lawns, and marshes. The woods are free from underwood of every kind and the trees are at such a distance from one another that the whole country or at least a great part of it might be cultivated without being obliged to cut down a single tree." And when he went on another trip to the south of the bay, he wrote afterward: "I found in many places a deep black soil which we thought was capable of producing any kind of grain . . . it produces beside timber as fine meadow as was ever seen."

In reality, Botany Bay bears little resemblance to Cook's descrip-

Botanists who sailed with Cook took great interest in the strange flowers and trees they found in all the new lands they visited. This drawing of the weeping bottlebrush is based on a sketch made by Sydney Parkinson near Cooktown, Queensland in 1770.

Above: the Great Barrier Reef is about 1,250 miles long and the largest coral reef in the world. Along the coast of Queensland parts of the reef are only 10 miles away from the mainland. It was through this channel that Cook tried to sail.

tion. No doubt he was influenced by Banks' botanical enthusiasm, but he nevertheless consistently overpraised Australia—the more so as he painfully groped his way along its eastern shore. In this he lacked the clinical detachment of Dampier, who found nothing worthwhile and said so.

Cook sailed the *Endeavour* northward, charting the coast as he went. After a few miles he passed a break a mile wide in the sandstone cliffs, named it Port Jackson and went on. Soon the *Endeavour* was within the treacherous reef-strewn line of the Great Barrier Reef—1,250 miles of perilous coral capable of tearing a ship to pieces. Cook navigated almost 1,000 miles within the reef before trouble struck. The leadsman had just sounded 17 fathoms (102 feet), when the *Endeavour*'s keel plowed and scraped into a projecting head of coral. Cook rushed on deck. For weeks the *Endeavour* had crawled forward a few yards at a time, boats ahead of it taking soundings, while men high in the rigging tried to spot the dark shadows in the water before the ship was on them. Cook had been

Right: only once in her long voyage did the gallant little *Endeavour* leak, after running aground on the Great Barrier Reef. Fortunately the crew were able to beach her, as shown here, and repair the hull. Within seven weeks she was seaworthy again.

expecting to meet trouble on the reefs and was prepared for it.

Quickly, *Endeavour*'s sails were lowered so that the keel would not be pulled farther over the coral. The ship was stuck under the port bow in only four feet of water with the tide running out, leaving it stranded. Now was the justification of Cook's choice of a collier. Its flat bottom kept it steady while a more conventional ship would have keeled over in such circumstances.

It seemed, at first, that the morning tide might lift the *Endeavour* clear. But the tide came in a foot lower, and, although the crew pulled on cables which had been anchored well out to sea during the night, the ship refused to budge. Cook tossed 40 to 50 tons overboard—six cannon (buoyed for later recovery), iron and stone ballast, casks, hoopstaves, oil jars, even some stores. But the *Endeavour* was stuck fast and had begun to leak. Pumps were manned constantly as captain and crew waited for the evening tide. Three pumps were not enough to cope and there was water four feet deep in the ship's bottom when it lifted on the tide.

Still they were not out of danger. The ship was safe in the shallow water, but if they sailed off the reef, it might sink in deeper seas. Cook decided to risk it. They "fothered" the ship—an intricate procedure by which a sail, filled with oakum, wool, rope ends, and dung,

is passed under the ship, then pulled tight in the hope that the suction of the water will draw the refuse as a plug into the leak. The ship's master had sighted a harbor where the ship could be repaired. It was the mouth of the Endeavour River, where Cooktown now stands. It took four days to get the ship into the harbor, and when it was finally beached they discovered that it was not the "fothering" that had saved it but an immense piece of coral plugging the largest of the holes.

For seven weeks, while they repaired the *Endeavour*'s hull, the

crew camped ashore and acquainted themselves with tropical Australia. They ate kangaroo, birds, mussels, fish, and countless turtles. The giant turtles weighed 300 pounds each and some of the mussels were so large that one made a full meal for two men. Cook even found some "greens" to balance the crew's diet. Then, after about a month, the inhabitants began to appear.

Some of the Aborigines became friendly enough to visit the ship. But it was an uneasy relationship, and within 24 hours of their visit they were burning the grass around the ship's shore camp. On August 6, Cook slowly moved the *Endeavour* out of the harbor. It took five days to get under way and immediately he found himself in the very worst part of the Great Barrier Reef. He could not risk another grounding, and decided to sail outside the coral.

"The moment we were without the breakers we had no ground with 100 fathoms of line, and found a large sea rolling in from the southeast. By this I was well assured we were got without all the shoals which gave us no small joy after having been intangled among islands and shoals, more or less, ever since the 26th of May in which

Above left: kangaroos looked very strange to the early European visitors, who marveled at their ability to leap to great heights and travel at speeds of up to 30 miles an hour. But the Europeans soon learned to catch them and eat them.
Above right: in Botany Bay, Cook and the ship's company of 94 had their first encounter with the Aborigines. Cook wrote in his journal, "As we approached the shore they all made off, except two men, who seemed resolved to oppose our landing." Both drawings are by Parkinson, who sailed with Cook.

time we have sailed above 360 leagues [about 1,100 miles] by the lead without ever having a leadsman out of the chains when the ship was under sail, a circumstance that perhaps never happened to any ship before."

But this joy was short-lived. The large sea "rolling in from the southeast" presented its own problems. The ship took very badly to the ocean exposure. Since he was also fearful of overshooting the passage between Australia and New Guinea, Cook resolved to return to the treacherous reefs.

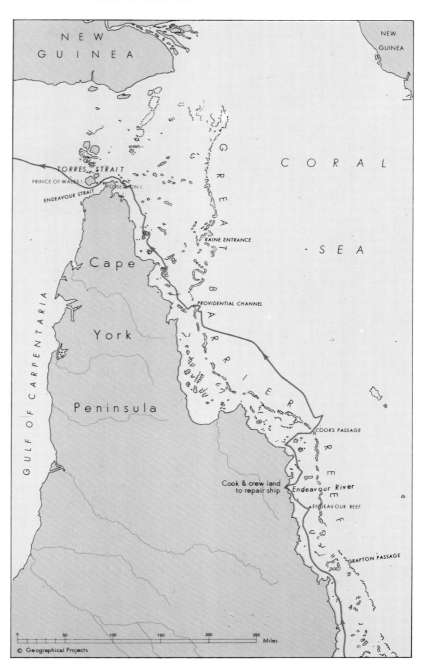

Right: the voyage of Captain Cook in the *Endeavour* up the east coast of what is now Queensland. The way in which Cook sailed in and out of the channel between the Great Barrier Reef and the mainland is clearly shown.

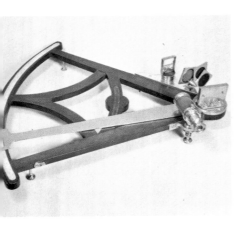

Modern scientific instruments mean that ships can be navigated accurately even under the most difficult weather conditions. For Cook, however, navigation was difficult and often inaccurate. Instruments like the quadrant (above) and the azimuth compass (above right) were useful but not always reliable.

As the *Endeavour* turned back toward the land, navigation became as haphazard as spinning a coin. Either the powerful trade wind blew the ship uncontrollably toward the reef, or there was calm and the current pulled them in. Sixty men at the boats were not strong enough to pull against the tide that swept in from the Pacific. And then, in the early hours of August 17, it seemed that disaster was finally upon them. Before dawn they could hear the roaring of the breakers on the nearby reef. As the sun came up, they could see less than a mile away to port "vast foaming breakers outlining the deadly wall of coral." There was a dead calm. The tide pulled the *Endeavour* inexorably toward destruction. They were only a few yards away from disaster, but still in water that was over 350 feet deep, when a breath of wind carried them back out to sea for a moment. The vessel had been so close to the wall of coral that the men on deck were drenched by the backlash of the breakers.

"The same sea that washed the side of the ship rose in a breaker prodigiously high the very next time it did rise," wrote Cook, "so that between us and destruction was only a dismal valley, the breadth of one wave, and even now no ground could be felt with 120 fathom. The pinnace [a small, light sailing vessel] was by this time patched up and hoisted out and sent ahead to tow. Still we had hardly any hopes of saving the ship, and full as little our lives, as we were full 10 leagues from the nearest land."

But the momentary breathing space provided by that solitary puff of wind off the land saved the *Endeavour*. Cook saw an opening in the reef through which an ebb tide was racing. He put the prow of

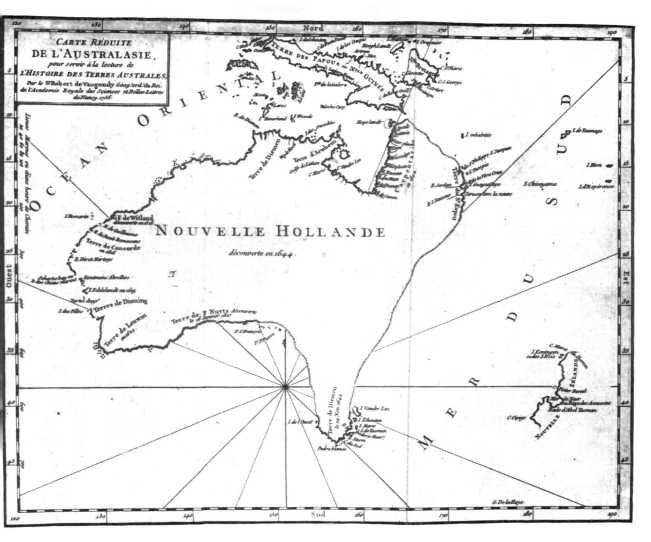

CARTE RÉDUITE
DE L'AUSTRALASIE,
pour servir à la lecture de
L'HISTOIRE DES TERRES AUSTRALES,
Par le Sr Robert de Vaugondy Géogr. ord. du Roi,
de l'Académie Royale des Sciences et Belles-Lettres
de Nancy. 1756.

OCÉAN ORIENTAL

NOUVELLE HOLLANDE

découverte en 1644.

MER DU SUD

MER DU SUD

Nord

Sud

Ouest

Est

the *Endeavour* into it and sailed through the narrow gap into the comparative safety and shelter inside the reef. "It is but a few days ago that I rejoiced at having got without the reef; but that joy was nothing . . . to what I now felt at being safe at an anchor within it."

Sailing slowly by day, anchoring by night, Cook made his way determinedly toward the Torres Strait. His log for Saturday, August 18, reveals the firmness of his purpose: "This doubtful point I had from my first coming upon the coast determined if possible to clear up. I now came to a fixed resolution to keep the mainland on board [within sight], let the consequence be what it will." He knew the importance of finding the strait. A direct route to the Spice Islands and to the Spanish possessions farther north would considerably enhance the value of the coast he had, in the last few months, so assiduously and painfully traced. He could not know that even today, 200 years later, the difficult navigation of the Torres Strait would preserve it as a little-used, one-way channel.

On August 21 and 22 Cook passed through the Torres Strait and found himself on a clear route to Batavia. Before leaving Australia,

Above: most up-to-date map used by Cook was this French map of 1756. It shows the northern and western coasts of Australia with the east and south sketched in where the cartographer thought they should be. New Zealand's two islands are shown as one, with the possibility of a large land mass attached. After Cook's voyage the entire coast of Australia was known and the two islands of New Zealand were mapped.

he went ashore and formally took possession of the whole eastern coast for Britain. He named his discovery New South Wales, in honor of King George's young son, the Prince of Wales.

What had Cook accomplished? As he wrote to John Walker, his friend and former employer, "I have made no very great discoveries, yet I have explored more of the Great South Sea than all who have gone before me, and little remains now to be done." Indeed, he went back to the Pacific for his second great voyage (1772–1775), cruised relentlessly over the ocean, and effectively removed *Terra Australis Incognita* from the maps so far as anything north of the Antarctic Circle was concerned.

Cook's achievement is, in fact, unsurpassed. Apart from disproving the southern land mass theory, he charted much of the

Pacific, established the true identity of New Zealand, disproved the Dutch assumption that New Holland was wholly a barren waste, and confirmed or rediscovered the Torres Strait. Cook also waged a constant battle against scurvy, the disease which had proved fatal on so many previous voyages of exploration. He strictly regulated his crew's diet and issued a daily supply of fresh vegetables or other foods containing the vital vitamin C. His success in virtually eliminating scurvy among his crew proved that ships could now travel great distances over long periods of time without undue loss of life. It was a turning point in maritime history. Cook remains one of the greatest explorers and leaders the world has known. He was probably its greatest navigator. King George III wept when he heard of Cook's death at the hands of Hawaiian savages on February 14, 1779.

Above: on his third voyage to the Pacific Ocean in the late 1770's, Captain Cook wintered in the shelter of the Hawaiian Islands. One of his ship's cutters was stolen. Trying to retrieve it Cook sealed the harbor, telling his men to prevent canoes from leaving. While he was ashore a canoe was fired upon and a chief was killed. News reached the native village just as Cook was leaving and the angry inhabitants attacked, which encouraged the English ships to fire their cannon. Cook tried to stop the cannon fire—"his humanity ... proved fatal to him ... having turned ... to give his orders to the boats, he was stabbed in the back, and fell with his face into the water."

Below: in the 1780's, a petition was made to the Prince of Wales asking him to use his influence to prevent convicts from being shipped to Australia. The Prince refused. This cartoon of the time shows the unpopular Prince being carried ashore at Botany Bay by a motley crew of contemporary political figures.

Early Colonization

4

British colonization of Australia was largely the result of American independence. When felons could no longer be shipped to Virginia, London's jails became dangerously overcrowded. As early as 1779, Joseph Banks had suggested that Botany Bay would make an ideal penal settlement. With the threat of another Great Plague unless something were done immediately, the government resolved to adopt Banks' suggestion.

In 1788, the British First Fleet, with 11 ships, 759 convicts, 211 soldiers, 30 wives, and 12 children, sailed into Botany Bay. They found a land dense with swamps, offering them neither shelter nor drinkable water. Captain Arthur Phillip, head of the expedition, immediately searched for a better site, and soon found the magnificent harbor that Cook had called Port Jackson, and which Phillip now christened Sydney Cove. He named it after Lord Sydney, the British home secretary at the time.

The colony's first huts were erected on the south shore of the harbor where Circular Quay now stands. In the early weeks after disembarkation, the convicts worked ashore by day and slept in the ships by night. Many tried to escape. But the land proved too hostile and the men always returned exhausted, hungry, and thirsty. It seemed that nothing eatable would grow in the arid soil, and in the

Above: since the 1500's English convicts had been held in anchored prison ships. In the 1800's many were transported to the American colonies, but after the War of Independence they were taken to Australian penal settlements.

Left: Australia's first settlers were dispatched to the new land as punishment for crimes such as stealing and assault. Even minor crimes were punished by the gallows and transportation was considered less drastic.

Above: Arthur Phillip (1738–1814) commanded the first shiploads of convicts to Australia. He became the first governor of New South Wales.

continued absence of fresh food most of the settlers fell ill with scurvy. Thunderstorms came to break the scorching midsummer heat. Dingoes ate the sheep. Six valuable cattle wandered off and were lost in the bush (areas of uncultivated scrub-covered land).

Nerves were frayed and tempers were short in the tiny colony—the Colony of Disgracefuls, they called it. The Aborigines watching from the bush saw savage floggings and many hangings. The commander of the marines had half his officers under arrest at one time. A man was hanged for stealing a bar of soap. But the colony survived. Even the arrival of the Second Fleet, with another 1,000 convicts to be housed and fed, did not overwhelm it. Gradually those "no-hopers" from Britain learned to master the difficult land.

During the first eight years the settlers never went far from Sydney. A few sailed up the inlet and built houses at Parramatta, but there was little or no real exploration. Only 100 miles of the coast had been examined, and that in the most cursory fashion. Then one day a man brought news of a great herd of wild cattle grazing on pastures finer than any yet seen, about 50 miles up the Nepean River. They were the descendants of the two bulls and four cows that had wandered away in the first months of the colony. The settlement's new governor, John Hunter, organized a party to examine the cattle. In the expedition was a young man, George Bass, who was

to contribute greatly to the next stage of Australian exploration.

George Bass was 24 years old when he arrived in Sydney. A surgeon on the ship that had brought Governor Hunter to the colony, Bass was a self-taught naturalist who was determined to explore this unknown territory. He brought a small sailing-boat, the *Tom Thumb*, from England, and within a few weeks of his arrival he made his first expedition. With him in the *Tom Thumb* was his servant, a boy called Martin, and Midshipman Matthew Flinders, a friend from the outwardbound voyage. Flinders, like Bass, was destined to make important contributions to Australia's further exploration.

Both Flinders and Bass were from Lincolnshire. Flinders, who was well educated, had planned a medical career. While still a young man, he was given a copy of Defoe's *Robinson Crusoe* and immediately decided to join the navy. At the age of 17 he sailed through the Torres Strait with William Bligh, captain of the *Bounty* and later governor of New South Wales. It took 19 days to come through the strait, and Flinders, charged with care of the chronometers and part of the chartwork, learned much from Bligh's skilled navigation. It was to stand him in good stead when he himself tackled the strait a decade later.

In 1795, Flinders and Bass took the 8-foot *Tom Thumb* south from Sydney Cove, through Botany Bay, and up the George's River.

Above: the Cowpastures on the Nepean River were an area of 60,000 acres about 30 miles from Sydney. A herd of wild cattle roamed the area, the off-spring of cows and bulls that strayed from the first settlement.

Above: Matthew Flinders (1774–1814) sailed through Bass Strait, proving that Tasmania is an island. He then went on to disprove the theory, popular at the time, that Australia and New South Wales were divided by a strait.

After eight days they returned to Port Jackson. For the first time since the settlement of the colony, two men had clearly showed themselves to be interested in exploration. Recognizing the importance of further discovery, Governor Hunter determined to encourage the two young men.

They went out again in March of the following year, this time in a colony-built boat, also dubbed the *Tom Thumb*. Their instructions were to explore a large river said to flow into the sea some miles south of Botany Bay. The expedition met with several mishaps. On the second day out their boat was thrown ashore by the heavy surf, and most of the cargo, including their weapons, was drenched. At one point, surrounded by hostile Aborigines, Flinders saved the day by volunteering to cut their beards. "I began with a large pair of scissors," he wrote afterward, "to execute my new office upon the eldest of four or five chins presented to me: and as great nicety was not required, the shearing of a dozen of them did not occupy me long."

The river was no more than a large inlet, Port Hacking. But they found a coal deposit, and again demonstrated that they were serious explorers worthy of a proper commission.

Governor Hunter soon provided an opportunity. On his first visit to Australia, he had noticed a strong easterly current and an "uncommon large sea" as he passed through latitude 40° south. He suspected that there existed "either a very deep gulf or a strait which may separate Van Diemen's Land from New Holland," and he was determined to find it. Such a discovery would save many days on the journey from India or the Cape to the young settlement at Port Jackson.

On December 3, 1797, Bass and a six-man crew sailed from Circular Quay, Sydney, in an open whale-boat provided by Hunter. Flinders, who had shipboard duties, was left behind. Bass carried provisions for 6 weeks, thus giving him enough food and water for an 11-week voyage, provided he was able to supplement his stores by occasional fishing and hunting.

In the face of terrible weather, Bass went as far as Western Port, parallel with the western end of Tasmania, before he was forced to turn back. In a journey lasting 12 weeks, he surveyed 600 miles of unexplored coast from an open boat. It was a feat which, as Flinders later noted, "has not perhaps its equal in the annals of maritime

Right: in his journal, Flinders describes how he and two companions weathered a storm in the tiny boat, *Tom Thumb*. "Mr. Bass kept the sheet of the sail in his hand . . .a single wrong movement, or a moment's inattention, would have sent us to the bottom. The task of the boy was to bale out the water which, in spite of every care, the sea threw in upon us."

Below: the Aborigines' attitude to the early settlers varied considerably. Here a party of Aborigines chase away a sailor collecting brushwood to light a camp fire.

history." Bass had not, on this voyage, proved conclusively that Van Diemen's Land was separated from the mainland. In 1798, however, when he and Flinders had circumnavigated the island, Flinders wrote to Hunter asking that the channel be named Bass Strait.

It was in September, 1798, that Flinders was given his first command, a 28-ton sloop, the *Norfolk*. With Bass and a crew of eight, he set out to establish positively that Van Diemen's Land was the island everyone now believed it to be. The *Norfolk* sailed from Port Jackson on October 7, with enough provisions for a three-month voyage. They stopped briefly at Twofold Bay to survey. Suddenly an Aborigine appeared. Flinders describes the encounter vividly:

"He was of middle age, unarmed, except with a whaddie [waddie] or wooden scimitar, and came up to us seemingly with careless confidence. We made much of him and gave him some biscuit; and he in return presented us with a piece of gristly fat, probably of whale. This I tasted; but watching an opportunity to spit it out when he should not be looking, I perceived him doing precisely the same thing with our biscuit, whose taste was probably no more agreeable to him, than his whale was to me." Flinders' party then started to set up their instruments for a trigonometric survey, whereupon "he quitted us, apparently satisfied that, from people who could thus occupy themselves seriously, there was nothing to be apprehended."

The *Norfolk* crossed to Van Diemen's Land via the Furneaux Islands and continued west to the mouth of the beautiful Tamar River. They explored the Tamar Valley and then went on. But as the coast turned northwest they began to fear that the "strait" was after all no more than a great gulf and that they were about to arrive back at Western Port. It was not until they noticed that low water came with the tide from the east and that the tide from the west bore every sign of springing from a large sea that they regained their confidence. The passage must exist, and they could not be far from it.

On December 9, the *Norfolk* turned south into the Indian Ocean. "So soon as we had passed the north sloping point, a long swell was perceived to come from the southwest, such as we had not been accustomed to for some time. It broke heavily upon all the western shores; but although it was likely to prove troublesome, and perhaps dangerous, Mr. Bass and myself hailed it with joy and mutual congratulation, as announcing the completion of our long wished for discovery of a passage into the Southern Indian Ocean."

Above: this map of the first British settlement, Port Jackson, was drawn by a transported convict. It was sent back to England where it was published and sold to people leaving for Australia.

Right: Adventure Bay in Tasmania. Around the coasts of Australia and New Zealand are some of the finest natural harbors in the world. Here Cook and other early explorers found safe and sheltered anchorage.

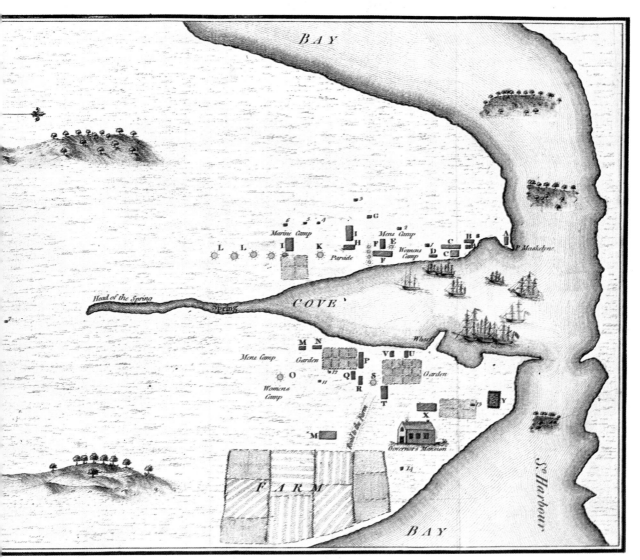

Above: Nicolas Baudin (1750(?)-1803) was sent to Australia by the French Republic to explore the south coast from Western Port along the coast to Nuyts Archipelago.

They sped around the west side of the island, spent Christmas exploring the Derwent River, and arrived in Port Jackson with a few stores left on January 11, 1799. Flinders and Bass had accomplished a good deal in their three-month voyage. Principally they had established Bass Strait and thus lopped off a week from the voyage to Sydney. But further, their exploration of the Tamar and the Derwent rivers was to lead to the setting up of new colonies at Launceston and Hobart.

For Bass it was the culmination of his career. He was a sick man and returned to England a few months later. But Flinders continued his exploration. He made a short winter trip up the east coast to search for a navigable river, but missed both the Brisbane and the Clarence. He returned convinced that "no river of importance intersected the East coast between the 24th and 39th degree of South latitude." One interesting incident occurred on the trip. Flinders had taken a Port Jackson Aborigine with him to act as interpreter. On going ashore at Moreton Bay—only six days sailing away—the man was unable to communicate with the local inhabitants. Flinders was being offered some early evidence of the 500 different languages of the Australian Aborigines.

Early the following year Flinders sailed for home determined to persuade the Admiralty to entrust him with the definitive circumnavigation, surveying, and charting of the whole of New Holland. He dedicated his *Observations on the coast of Van Diemen's Land*

Left: one of the officers sailing with Baudin took with him an apparatus for distilling water which he hoped would solve the problem of fresh drinking water aboard ship. The transformation of seawater was a long process and was carried out by a few men on shore, while the rest worked on the ship or hunted game for fresh food to eat.

Australia's wild flowers are hardy plants and many grow in the interior desert and wilderness regions. This is *Grevillea Banksii*. The drawing is by Bauer, one of the two artists who sailed to Australia with Flinders on board the *Investigator*.

to Sir Joseph Banks, who as President of the Royal Society was then the most politically powerful man in science. Flinders wrote to Banks, outlining his ambition. It was a fascinating letter, full of the conjecture that would most whet Banks' interest—"probably it will be found that an extensive strait separates New South Wales from New Holland by the way of the Gulf of Carpentaria; or perhaps a southern gulf may only peninsulate New South Wales."

Banks retained a keen interest in the land which he, as a young man, had helped to discover. Within a few days of his meeting with Flinders, the Admiralty had directed the Navy Board to ready a ship for the voyage. The vessel was provisioned for six months and renamed the *Investigator*. The speed of their decision was due, largely, to increased French interest in the South Pacific. Already Nicolas Baudin and Emmanuel Hamelin had been sent to explore the unknown south coast of New Holland on behalf of the French government. Britain was anxious to establish her claim to the Australian continent.

Two months after his first meeting with Banks, Flinders was able to assume command and begin his log. It was already late January and he had less than 11 months to reach Australia if he was to take full advantage of the southern summer. Things did not go well at first. In taking the *Investigator* from southeast England to Portsmouth, Flinders ran her aground in the Channel and several prisoners placed in his charge escaped. His bride, newly installed aboard ship,

Above: Kangaroos and other Australian animals were studied carefully by the scientists who traveled with the early explorers. They learned that a kangaroo is an inch long at birth but can grow as tall as 7 feet. The young kangaroo spends the first few months of life in its mother's pouch.

was asked to leave when Admiralty officials found her in the captain's cabin without her bonnet—an unequivocal indication that she regarded herself as "at home." Finally, accompanied by an astronomer, a naturalist, two artists, a miner, a gardener, and a folding conservatory for plant specimens, the *Investigator* sailed from England on July 17, 1801. Flinders' instructions were to "proceed in her to the coast of New Holland for the purpose of making a complete examination and survey of the said coast."

The *Investigator* reached Cape Leeuwin on December 6. Flinders hurried on to King George Sound where he stayed for four weeks while repairing the *Investigator* for its gigantic task. The day of departure was one of great ceremony. The embarkation of the marines, particularly, delighted the Aborigine observers. "The red coats with white crossed belts were so much in their way of ornamenting themselves that they absolutely screamed with delight on seeing the men drawn up," wrote Flinders. "The fife, the drum, the motion of the exercise, all excited curiosity and astonishment. To the exercise they paid the most earnest silent attention. Several of them moved their hands involuntarily according to the motion, and an old man placed himself at the end of a rank with a short staff which he shouldered, presented, and grounded, as did the marines their muskets."

Thus began the task of charting the southern coast of Australia. Every day, Flinders went ashore, taking measurements and surveying. The ship's progress was slow, and there were days when he would walk 20 miles to the top of the highest hill to be sure of the best bearings. From Nuyts Archipelago, Flinders was following virgin coast, and his examination of the shoreline became even more intense. One of the mysteries of New Holland and New South Wales—as the west and east coasts were known—was that no major river had yet been found emptying into the sea. It was inconceivable that a land mass of this size should not be drained by a large river, unless the two coasts were actually separated into islands or contained a great inland sea. In either case, the separating channel or the entrance to the sea must exist, and the virgin south coast from Nuyts Archipelago to Western Port must offer it.

As he rounded Cape Catastrophe—so named because here eight members of his crew were drowned—Flinders found himself in the finest harbor in South Australia. Following the coast northward for 180 miles, it seemed he had found, at last, the strait he was looking for. But gradually its sides narrowed, and the inlet ended in mud flats. Flinders turned the *Investigator* southward and sailed down the other shore. It was neither a strait, nor an entrance to an inland sea, but a great gulf. He named it Spencer Gulf after the First Lord of the Admiralty who had originally agreed to his project. It took 15 days to travel up the west side and down the east side of Spencer Gulf. Flinders replenished his food stores on Kangaroo Island.

Late in the afternoon of April 8, as the *Investigator* sailed eastward across a broad sandy bay, the lookout reported a white rock ahead. As they drew nearer, the "rock" was seen to be a ship, and at six o'clock was identified as Nicolas Baudin's *Géographe*. It was an astonishing coincidence that the two discovery ships, both following

Every expedition included an artist who recorded sights the explorers saw. This sketch by Petit, who sailed with Baudin, must have given Europeans one of their first views of an Aborigine.

75

a virgin coastline over 12,000 miles from home, should meet at the last point of the continent to be discovered, the very point that all had been looking for. It is here that Australia's large river, the Murray, drains into the sea.

That evening and the following morning, Flinders went aboard Baudin's ship. He outlined his work from Cape Leeuwin and Baudin told of his journey through the Bass Strait. The French captain did not realize he was talking to the Flinders whose name was on the chart he had been using. The most remarkable feature about the meeting in Encounter Bay was that both captains missed the entrance to the Murray River. Had they found it they would have solved .the mysterious problem of Australia's inland drainage. If this estuary had been discovered in 1802, it might also have changed the shape of Australian history throughout the first half of the 1800's.

On April 9, the two ships went their separate ways. As Flinders coasted eastward he wrote in the French names to fill in his charts. He reached Cape Otway and was blown by gales over to King Island. He regained the mainland coast five days later and sailed into Port Phillip Bay on April 26, 1802. But he was second-comer. Ten weeks before, Lieutenant John Murray, commander of the *Lady Nelson*, had found the huge harbor on which Melbourne now stands. Flinders examined the harbor thoroughly, then, in six days, raced through the Bass Strait, around Cape Howe and was in Port Jackson on May 8.

The first leg of his expedition had been most successful. He had sailed more than 20,000 miles since leaving England and in five months he had surveyed New Holland from Cape Leeuwin to Port

Left: Australian explorers found that, like the natives of Africa and America, the Aborigines loved to trade directions and food for glass beads and other trinkets. They rowed out to passing ships in the hopes of being given some of the white man's treasure. Here Murray Island natives row out to greet Matthew Flinders.

Jackson. Remarkably, everyone on board remained in good health.

The *Investigator* proceeded from Port Jackson on July 22 to complete the circumnavigation. Flinders' plan was to examine the coast from Hervey Bay to the beginning of the Great Barrier Reef, explore the passage through the Torres Strait, examine the Gulf of Carpentaria, and sail the length of the north and northwest coast. It was an enormous program. As Flinders put it: "Cook had reaped the harvest of discovery, but the gleanings of the field remained to be gathered." It was expected that the remainder of the expedition would take almost a year.

Above: the coast of Queensland. Seeing the lush, green tropical jungle that came right down to the shore, explorers had no way of knowing that much of the interior of the continent was arid desert.

Right: sailing in wooden ships, early sailors had to be on the watch for rotting timbers, leaks, and numerous other faults in the ship's hull. Here a ship has been beached and tilted to one side, so that the hull can be scraped clean and repaired.

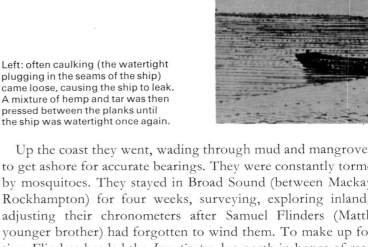

Left: often caulking (the watertight plugging in the seams of the ship) came loose, causing the ship to leak. A mixture of hemp and tar was then pressed between the planks until the ship was watertight once again.

Up the coast they went, wading through mud and mangrove trees to get ashore for accurate bearings. They were constantly tormented by mosquitoes. They stayed in Broad Sound (between Mackay and Rockhampton) for four weeks, surveying, exploring inland, and adjusting their chronometers after Samuel Flinders (Matthew's younger brother) had forgotten to wind them. To make up for lost time Flinders headed the *Investigator* due north in hopes of reaching the open sea and avoiding the Great Barrier Reef. But the *Investigator* was soon trapped in the shoals and deadly coral. For 12 days they sailed above the reef, surrounded by breakers and finding no end to the danger however far they struck eastward. On October 11, Flinders abandoned his plan and turned back to the mainland. From here he hugged the shore northward, well inside the barrier of the reef, until north of Cumberland Islands he found a way out into the Pacific.

Flinders entered the Torres Strait with only four days to go before the beginning of the monsoon season. With a ship decayed below the waterline and leaking at least 10 inches an hour, there could be only disaster if he hit the coral now. Flinders was the ninth known commander to take a ship through the strait but the first to go wholly in search of a safe passage. In 1792, Bligh had taken 19 days to find a way through. Having discovered the best

route, Prince of Wales Channel, Flinders did it in six days. He calculated it could be done in three days and proved it in the *Cumberland* a year later. But his prediction that ships could now use this route, thus reducing the sailing time from the Pacific to India by at least five weeks, assumed a virtually nonexistent breed of captains with his own skill and courage. The route, for all its shortness, was, and still is, too difficult and dangerous to be generally adopted.

Armed with the old Dutch charts, Flinders now advanced down the east coast of the Gulf of Carpentaria—the route of the *Duyfken* almost 200 years earlier. He was looking for the strait that would cut off New Holland from New South Wales. After passing the head of the gulf, he concluded that there was no strait in the north just as there had been none in the south. In fact, his conclusion was but a lucky guess. Just as he had missed the Murray River on the south coast, and the Brisbane on the east, so here he bypassed the Norman, the Bynoe, and the Flinders. Although he kept closer to the shoreline than any sea explorer before him, he had the misfortune of missing every major Australian river.

In the deadening heat of the Gulf, Flinders was compelled to halt his ship for repairs. The *Investigator* was leaking badly and needed caulking if she were to continue the journey. But, on

Below: every ship in an expedition carried a skilled carpenter as a member of the crew. Equipped with hot tar, a saw, and other tools, he was expected to carry out any necessary repairs during the voyage.

examining her off Sweers Islands, timber after timber was found to be rotten or rotting. The master and the carpenter reported on its condition: "From the state to which the ship now seems to be advanced, it is our joint opinion that in 12 months there will scarcely be a sound timber in her; but that if she remains in fine weather and happens no accident, she may run six months longer without much risk."

The news was a profound disappointment to Flinders. He was still only 16 months out of England on a voyage that should have

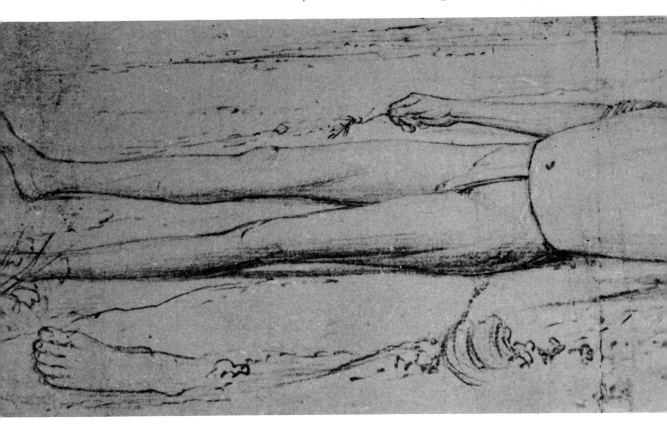

lasted four years. On November 26, 1802, he wrote in his journal: "From this dreadful state of the ship, I find the complete examination of this extensive country, which is one of the nearest objects to my heart, to be greatly impeded, if not wholly frustrated."

Four days later, however, Flinders set sail up the western shore of the Gulf as though nothing had happened. Once he struck rock three times in quick succession but there was no apparent damage and he sailed on. He hugged the coast as daringly as before, discovering "capes" charted by the Dutch to be in reality islands or island groups separated from the mainland Throughout his entire survey, Flinders rarely stood more than five miles off the coast, using as his yardstick of proximity his ability to see the surf washing on the shore.

Shortly after Christmas he reached Groote Eylandt, the large island off the west coast of Arnhem Land. In Blue Mud Bay, the explorers found several human skeletons standing upright in the hollow stumps of trees, the skulls and bones smeared with red and white paint. They also saw cave paintings of porpoises, turtles, kangaroos, and even a human hand. There were narrative paintings, too, of turtle and kangaroo hunts, done in charcoal.

On Groote Eylandt the *Investigator*'s crew clashed with the inhabitants. The Aborigines would pretend friendship, walking arm-in-arm with the sailors, then suddenly snatch some booty and run off into

Left: Flinders had issued orders that Aborigines were not to be shot. But after an attack on one of his men at Blue Mud Bay shots were fired and one Aborigine died. An artist on board drew a sketch of the dead man.

Below: Flinders named one island after Probasso, shown here, the commander of a fleet of Malay proas he encountered. The Malays had sailed from Macassar to the northern coast of Australia to fish for *trepang* (sea cucumber) which they could sell to the Chinese.

the bush. It was a game that had to be tolerated, for Flinders had issued strict instructions regarding conduct toward the "Indians." Everything must be endured short of a spear attack. But one day on Groote Eylandt a deliberate attack on a party of sailors took place and the master's mate received four spear wounds. For the first time guns were used to force the Aborigines to retreat.

February came, and over a third of the *Investigator*'s allotted time had elapsed. But when he came out of the Gulf, Flinders could not resist the shoreline of Arnhem. He fixed the position of Cape Arnhem and had conversations with the captains of six Malay proas whom he met fishing for trepang (sea cucumber). On March 5, he made his last survey in a whale-boat on Arnhem Bay.

Flinders was only 29, but he was a weary and disappointed man. Hardly able to walk for the ulcers on his feet, he at last consented

> I undersigned, captain in His Britannic Majesty's navy, having obtained leave of his Excellency the captain-general to return in my country by the way of Bengal, Promise on my word of honour not to act in any service which might be considered as directly or indirectly hostile to France or its Allies, during the course of the present war
>
> Port Napoleon, Isle de France, 7th June 1810
>
> (Signed) Mattw. Flinders

Above: Flinders' hopes of returning to England in glory were interrupted by the French when he was imprisoned in Mauritius. Over six years later he was released to return to England after he had signed a letter, shown above, promising not to take part in the war that was raging between France and England.

to set sail for home. His route took him first across the Arafura Sea to the port of Kupang, on the island of Timor. With less than two months of the *Investigator's* predicted life span still remaining, he charted a course for Sydney. Although he made record time on the return voyage, Flinders' men were ill and before he sailed into Port Jackson on July 9, five of the crew had died.

Flinders set off for home anxious to obtain a new ship and complete his mapping of the remaining quarter of the continent. But luck was against him and the ship on which he had booked passage was shipwrecked on the Great Barrier Reef. Eventually he got back to Sydney and was given the only available boat, a 29-ton schooner, the *Cumberland*, to make the 13,000-mile journey back to England. He went through the Torres Strait in three days, but the ship was leaking so badly he was forced to put in at Mauritius. There he was imprisoned by the French, who were still at war with Britain. He spent six and a half years in a Mauritius jail, while the French claimed his discoveries as their own. When he got back to England he was a broken man. He would never travel again.

For four years Flinders worked on his book, *A Voyage to Terra Australis*, and died on the day in 1814 when it was published. "Had I permitted myself," he wrote in the book, "any innovation upon the original term [Terra Australis], it would have been to convert it into Australia, as being more agreeable to the ear, and an assimilation to the names of the other great portions of the earth."

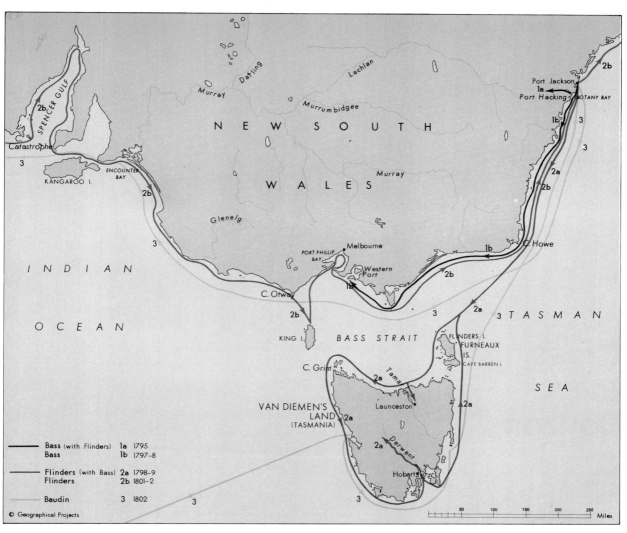

Above: voyages of Flinders, Bass, and
Baudin around the coasts of southern
Australia and Van Diemen's Land
(Tasmania). Flinders and Bass
undertook the first serious exploration
of southern Australia, and were
responsible for surveying the coastline
and for proving that Van Diemen's
Land was an island. Later, Flinders and
Baudin made explorations of more of
the Australian coastline.

Crossing the Horizon

5

A quarter of a century after the arrival of the First Fleet, the Australian settlers still had not ventured far from the small colony at Sydney. Forty miles to the west were the Blue Mountains—an encircling wall of precipitous ridges that defied every attempt by the colonists to break out. The young colony had to find a way over this barrier before the great continent could be explored.

Two marines, Dawes and Johnston, from the First Fleet's flagship *Sirius*, attempted a breakthrough in the colony's early years. In 1793, William Paterson sought a water route through the mountains. After carrying his boat over five steep waterfalls in the space of 10 miles, he too admitted defeat. Finally, Henry Hacking, an experienced bushman (the name given to Australian frontiersmen) attempted the crossing. He had passed 20 ridges and could still see nothing but mountains when he reported: "There is no hope of extending civilization beyond the present settlements."

The impenetrability of the Blue Mountains soon gave rise to legends, especially among the convicts of Sydney. They dreamed of a world of white people on the other side, of being free and enjoying the comforts of life without work and hardship. Some thought the

mountains offered an easy escape route to China. None of the prisoners got through, but many tried. Eventually, Governor Hunter felt it essential to dispel these myths if the colony was to maintain discipline among the convicts. He sent John Wilson, a white renegade who had "gone bush," which meant he had escaped to live off the land, across the mountains. Wilson made two expeditions in January and March, 1798. He was away just under a month on each trip, exploring 250 miles on the first and 350 miles on the second. He got as far as Goulburn to the southwest and found a big sluggish river, possibly the Lachlan.

It began to seem that no one would cross this strange wilderness. Then, in 1813, Gregory Blaxland approached the new governor, Lachlan Macquarie, with an ingenious plan to conquer the mountains. His predecessors had all followed the valleys until they came up against dead ends. Blaxland's plan was to stay on the ridge tops.

Blaxland set out on May 11, 1813, from his farm at Penrith on the Nepean River. He was accompanied by William Lawson, William Charles Wentworth, 4 convicts, and 24 horses. Some days the expedition made no more than 2 miles. On May 31, the men saw

Charles Sturt looking out over a stony desert in the Australian interior. Early settlers at Sydney, especially the convicts, believed that a paradise lay in the interior of the new continent, on the other side of the Blue Mountains. But although the first explorers did find some fine grassland, they also discovered that much of the country's interior was barren desert.

For some years the Blue Mountains prevented settlers from traveling inland from Sydney, and it was not until 1813 that they were crossed by Gregory Blaxland. The mountain range is covered with eucalyptus trees, and the fine drops of oil in the atmosphere often give the trees a bluish haze. This haze gave the mountains their name.

mile upon mile of rich, green, well-watered country opening before them. Blaxland was a rancher whose pasturelands in the thickly wooded confine by the sea were no longer large enough to support his herds. Now, from Mount York, he could see land "sufficient to support the stock of the colony for the next 30 years." Excitedly the party descended into the valley. The horses grazed on the luxurious grass, while the men banqueted on kangaroo and fish. Although they had not crossed the main range, Blaxland and his party had knocked a large hole in the wall that had surrounded the "Colony of Disgracefuls" for 25 years.

Macquarie did not announce Blaxland's discovery immediately. He did not want large numbers of people pouring into the valley at one time. First, he sent an experienced surveyor, George Evans, to confirm Blaxland's findings. From Mount York, Evans continued down the Fish and the Macquarie rivers over grassy plains for 20 miles beyond the present site of Bathurst. In 1815, exploring deeper into the west, Evans found the Lachlan River. His findings supported those of Blaxland, and the governor engaged William Cox to build a road. With the promise of freedom at the end, convict labor constructed 101 miles of road in 6 months. By 1815, Macquarie himself was able to travel to Bathurst in style.

In 1817, the surveyor general, John Oxley, began the exploration of the interior. He led an expedition down the Lachlan, but unwittingly picked the wettest winter for years. Where, at any other time,

he would have been walking over fine pastureland, he found himself bogged down in swamp and marshland. The following winter Oxley took a party northwest down the Macquarie River. Again he fought his way through miles of swamp. The horses sank to their bellies, and the men waded waist-deep in the quagmire. He concluded that he could not be far from the inland sea which was still the commonly held explanation of inland drainage. When he could penetrate no farther west, he turned to the east and there discovered the rich pastures of the Liverpool Plains. Crossing the Great Dividing Range with its 3,000-foot-deep ravines, one of his horses literally burst with the exertion of the climb. The party emerged on the coast near Port Macquarie, over 200 miles north of Sydney.

Oxley had found acres of fertile land desperately needed by the growing colony. The character of Sydney was changing rapidly. All restrictions on free emigration had been removed by the British government in 1816, and thousands of Englishmen rushed to the new country. Space was urgently needed to accommodate these newcomers. News of the rich land to the west was eagerly received, but an easier route across the Great Dividing Range had to be found.

Allan Cunningham, an English botanist, set out to find the easy exit to the north that had eluded Oxley. In 1823, he found Pandora's Pass leading into the Liverpool Plains. Cunningham himself was too weak from his journey to go through the pass, but within a

After a way had been found across the Blue Mountains the next problem was how to transport the supplies and materials needed for starting a new settlement. So, with the abundance of free labor provided by the convicts, a road was built from Sydney to Bathurst.

Above: a shipload of settlers bound for Australia leaving Britain in the 1800's. When the first settlement was founded only convicts and military personnel lived in Australia. But as more and more men were needed to build roads and farm newly-explored land the British government began to encourage free men and their families to emigrate. They offered prospective settlers positions of responsibility with convicts for servants, but in 1819 there were still five times as many convicts as free men and women.

year eager stockmen were driving their cattle along his trail. Four years later, with the mountains on his right, Cunningham trekked almost to Brisbane, discovering on the Darling Downs what was soon to be the richest sheep and cattle country in the world.

Hamilton Hume, born at Parramatta, was Australia's first native-born explorer. In 1824, with William Hovell, he led a party to explore the land between Sydney and the south coast. Hume and Hovell were the first white men to cross the Murrumbidgee and the Murray rivers. The party was plagued by leeches and ticks, flies and mosquitoes, and the men quarreled continually. After two months, they reached the coast at Geelong, a few miles west of what is now Melbourne. Then, urged on by hostile Aborigines, they made the return trip in half the time of the outward journey.

Still the growing colony needed more land. Sydney's new governor, Ralph Darling, selected 33-year-old Captain Charles Sturt, a member of his military secretariat, to find it. Sturt's commission was to discover the secret of the drainage of New South Wales' rivers. Oxley had been bogged down by swamps near the Lachlan River. Sturt reasoned that because it was now the dry season, the swamps would be passable. With Hamilton Hume, two soldiers, and eight convicts, Sturt followed the Macquarie River far

beyond the spot where Oxley had watched it disappear into the marshes. Twelve-foot-high reeds blocked much of their path. Often the Aborigines set fire to the reeds a few yards ahead of them to hinder their passage. The sun blazed down, blistering their faces and inflaming their eyes. Leeches clung to their legs and kangaroo flies bit their flesh. They squeezed river mud through handkerchiefs to get drops of water to slake their thirst. Hostile Aborigines tracked them wherever they went. Sturt and his party were experiencing what was to become a familiar pattern for all those who dared to seek out the secrets of this vast land.

Right: Charles Sturt, a young army officer, had the knowledge and sense of adventure needed to start land exploration in the new colony. Born in India, he had traveled to Ireland, France, Spain, and Canada before going to Australia with his regiment.

Below: this cartoon satirizes the attempt by the British government in the 1800's to stabilize the new colony by encouraging unmarried women to emigrate to Australia.

Above: Aborigines beside the Murray River. On his expedition down the river Sturt described them as "the worst-featured of any I had ever seen. It is scarcely possible...that human beings could be so hideous and loathsome." As the party traveled farther downstream the Aborigines became increasingly hostile.

In February, 1829, Sturt wrote: "We suddenly found ourselves on the banks of a noble river—the channel of the river was from 70 to 80 yards broad and enclosed an unbroken sheet of water, evidently very deep, and literally covered with pelicans and other wild fowl." It was the Darling. But the water was salt. They went 80 miles downstream where the river broadened, but the water remained salt. It was clear from the height of the Darling's banks that "furious torrents must sometimes rage in it." But what happened to it when it was full? "Its course is involved in mystery," wrote Sturt. "Does it make its way to the south coast or exhaust itself in feeding a succession of swamps in the centre of the island?"

Later in the same year, Sturt set out again to find the solution to the drainage riddle. This time he went down the Murrumbidgee River with a young red-headed naturalist, George Macley. They floated a 27-foot whale-boat on the river and within a week were at the Murray. Sturt described the Aborigines they met en route as "the worst-featured of any I had ever seen. It is scarcely possible to conceive that human beings could be so hideous and loathsome." In other places he saw young men "cleaner than most" and old men standing "exceedingly erect." But the women and children were diseased and ill-fed. The women were often left to get their own food or take what was nonchalantly thrown to them by the men. Sturt observed their customs: "The old men alone have the privilege of eating the emu. This evidently is a law of policy and necessity for if the emus were allowed to be indiscriminately slaughtered they would soon become extinct. Civilized nations may learn a wholesome lesson even from savages, as in this instance of their forbearance. For somewhat similar reasons perhaps, married people alone are here permitted to eat ducks."

The party made friends with many of the Aborigines. One group of tribesmen came and slept by their campfire. "Macley's extreme good humour had made a most favourable impression upon them, and I can picture him even now," wrote Sturt, "joining in their wild song. Whether it was from his entering so readily into their mirth or from anything peculiar that struck them, the impression upon the whole of us was that they took him to have been originally a black in consequence of which they gave him the name of Rudi."

But, as Sturt and his men traveled down the Murray, Aborigines they passed became increasingly hostile. Finally, on a spit in the

river, 600 angry tribesmen massed to halt the invaders. "We approached so near that they held their spears quivering in their grasp ready to hurl. They were painted in various ways. Some, who had marked their ribs and thighs and faces with a white pigment, looked like skeletons, others were daubed over with red and yellow ochre and their bodies shone with the grease with which they had besmeared themselves."

Sturt prepared to fight. But before he could fire on the cluster of Aborigines, Macley stopped him. Four warriors were hurrying toward the angry group. One went ahead and, when he reached the sandbank, succeeded in persuading the Aborigines to lay down their arms. After their providential rescue, Sturt noticed that they were at the junction of another river. Accompanied by the now friendly Aborigines they rowed up the new river for a few miles until Sturt was convinced that this was where the Darling, the river he had explored earlier, flowed into the Murray.

Sturt then turned and continued down the Murray for about 400 miles. They finally reached the shallows of Lake Alexandrina which earlier coastal explorers had not recognized as the mouth of a great river. The men could hear the thunder of the sea from Encounter Bay. But sandbanks and quicksands made it impossible to sail the boat to the sea. They were too weak to carry the boat, and too exhausted to walk over the mountains to St. Vincent Gulf. There was nothing to do but turn back and row the 1,000 miles upstream

Sturt's journey down the Murray River (above), to its mouth at Lake Alexandrina opened up new and fertile lands to the settlers, as well as being largely responsible for solving the mystery of Australia's inland drainage.

for home. Their food supply was dangerously low. Even by carefully rationing the tea and damper (a cooked mixture of flour and water), Sturt realized that their supplies would not hold out.

It seemed an impossible task. One man lost his senses. Sturt went partially blind. The men grew so tired that they no longer bothered to set the nightlines for fish. Others fell asleep rowing. The farther upstream they pulled, the stronger the downstream current became, until in one spot they were stationary. And all the time they were harassed by unfriendly Aborigines.

The party was ready to accept defeat when they reached the rapids and found themselves without the strength to lift the boat over the rocks. In pouring rain they stood up to their shoulders in the cascading river vainly struggling to lift the boat into still water. Groups of Aborigines, armed with spears, began to surround them. Suddenly Sturt saw the warrior who had saved them before. He beckoned to him and soon a party of Aborigines had lifted the boat clear of the rocks. The journey continued.

It was on April 12, 1830, that Sturt sent the two strongest men on foot to Wantabadgery, 90 miles away, for relief. The two made the return trip in seven days, sinking to the ground with exhaustion and pain when they got back. They were just in time. The last ounce of flour was being weighed out.

Sturt's exploration had finally liberated the new settlers. He brought back tales of the richness of the Murray Valley. Within only two years of his ordeal, 9 ranches, or stations, had spread 50 miles down the Murrumbidgee. Before his journey, land was

Left: the junction of the Murray and Darling rivers, another of Sturt's discoveries. Because of his courageous efforts to open the Australian interior Sturt is often called the "father of Australian discovery."

scarce and most of it was in the hands of a few men. Sturt's expedition brought land and water within the reach of every colonist.

The following year, Sir Thomas Livingstone Mitchell followed in Sturt's path. Mitchell doubted that the Darling emptied into the Murray. There was rumor of a great river to the north of the Liverpool Plains. Leading 15 convicts, Mitchell set out to settle all doubts. He reached the MacIntyre River, a tributary of the Upper Darling, before tragedy halted him and turned his party back to Sydney. Having gone ahead with the main party, he had left three men to follow up with fresh provisions about the time his supplies would be exhausted. But only one man arrived, and empty-handed. His two companions had been murdered by Aborigines and the supplies plundered. Mitchell sank his boat and set off for home with the little food that was left. He made a detour to visit the murder

Above: white men, traveling into the unknown, had other problems as well as the shortage of water. In one area the Aborigines would be friendly and helpful, exchanging directions and food for trinkets, but a few miles down the river they could be hostile and even warlike.

Below: often a native tribe, armed and aggressive, could be distracted from their thoughts of attack by presents such as glass beads and colored cloth. Even the simple banging of two cups could save the day as the natives heard the rhythm and started to dance.

Above: Sir Thomas Mitchell (1792-1855) was not only a great explorer but he served as a pioneer surveyor. He laid out some of Australia's first towns, planned some of the country's early roads, and supervised bridge building.

camp and was met by the horrible sight of four human legs sticking out from a pile of rubbish. The air was heavy with the smell of decaying flesh. He and his men buried their two comrades and returned to Sydney.

In 1835, Mitchell tried again. This time he went along the Bogan River for about 100 miles, then across to the Darling and continued down river to within 150 miles of its junction with the Murray, before hostile Aborigines again forced him to turn back. Earlier, one of his party, Richard Cunningham, had strayed from the camp and wandered alone for days. Delirious, he was found by a tribe of Aborigines who stabbed him to death with their spears. On the Darling, the party was involved in a fight in which a number of Aborigines were killed, including a woman with a child. To go on was impossible.

On March 17, 1836, Mitchell made his third attempt to solve the riddle of the rivers. He was convinced now that Sturt had mistaken

Left: the Murrumbidgee River is typical of the rivers traveled by the pioneers. The subtropical vegetation reached down to the river and back as far as the eye could see. Strange noises could be heard as unseen animals called to one another, and explorers were aware of being watched by unseen natives.

Right: some of the Aborigines attached themselves to the strangers with the pale skin who were entering their land. They acted as guides as well as helping the pioneers to find fresh water and food. One of the best known native guides was Tarandurey whose daughter, Ballandella, was raised with Mitchell's children.

the Lachlan for the Darling. With 24 men dressed like soldiers in red shirts and white braces, he set off down the Lachlan. Behind them trailed a hundred sheep which would serve as their main food supply. Soon after starting they picked up an Aborigine woman, a widow with a child of four, to act as a guide. The little girl, who was called Ballandella, soon became a great favorite in the camp.

Mitchell realized he was wrong about the Lachlan when he found it flowing into the Murrumbidgee. There was nothing to do but follow the river down to the Murray and examine for himself the river which Sturt had called the Darling. But again, trouble lay ahead. Friendly Aborigines warned Mitchell that the tribe his men had attacked the previous year was on its way to seek revenge. When they suddenly appeared, the tribe seemed friendly enough, merely asking for compensation for the children of those killed. But Mitchell suspected that the Aborigines were plotting revenge. Suddenly, they attacked, and in the ensuing battle, seven Aborigines were killed. On his return to Sydney, a court of inquiry censured Mitchell for his slaying of the seven men. Today the censure seems a mild punishment but at the time, despite the official government policy always to deal well with the Aborigines, it was considered severe.

After the battle, Mitchell hurried up the Darling. When he saw the river flowing in from the north, he could not doubt that it was the same river he had traveled the previous year. Sturt had been correct. The mystery of the drainage of southeast Australia was finally cleared up. There was no inland sea.

Above: an expedition on the Murrumbidgee River. The early explorers of Australia who sailed round the coast had failed to find any great rivers flowing out into the sea. For this reason, the idea of an inland sea had grown up. In the 1830's Mitchell traced the Murrumbidgee, the Darling, and the Lachlan, and finally disproved the inland sea theory.

Left: the government had announced that any white man killing a native would have to answer to the courts, as would a native who killed a white man. But the Aborigines could not read, so picture posters like these were displayed around the settlements.

Right: southeastern Australia, showing the routes of the explorers of this corner of the vast continent during the period from 1813 to 1845.

Hoping to justify his expedition with some positive finding, Mitchell decided to turn back up the Murray and then trek southward to the coast. Before long his party was walking over some of the finest land the men had ever seen. At last, Mitchell appeared to have made a discovery.

Eventually the expedition stumbled on a river, the Glenelg, broad enough to launch the boat that had been carried nearly 300 miles. They sailed down to the sea at Discovery Bay. While there, the widow approached Mitchell, white circles painted around her

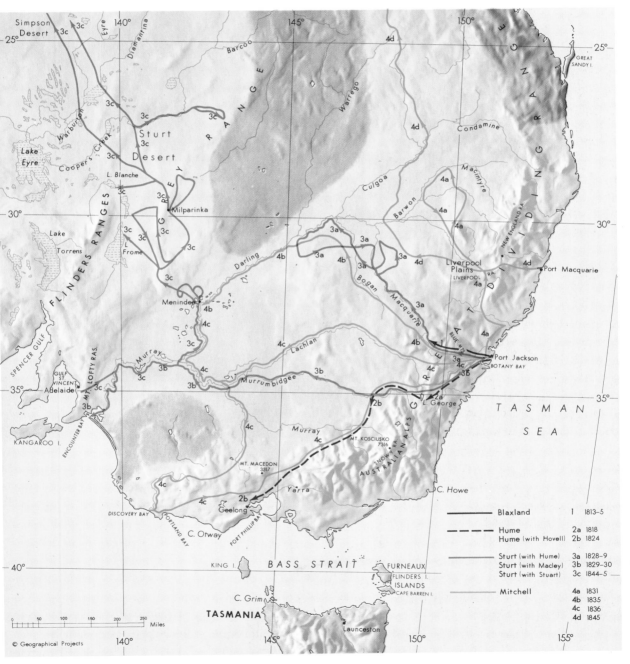

	Blaxland	1	1813–5
	Hume	2a	1818
	Hume (with Hovell)	2b	1824
	Sturt (with Hume)	3a	1828–9
	Sturt (with Macley)	3b	1829–30
	Sturt (with Stuart)	3c	1844–5
	Mitchell	4a	1831
		4b	1835
		4c	1836
		4d	1845

© Geographical Projects

The British first claimed Tasmania in 1788, and a settlement was established at the mouth of the Derwent River in 1803. In the following year the settlement was moved upstream to the present site of Hobart, as shown here.

eyes in mourning. She had determined to give her child to him. Ballandella had long since been weaned from her normal diet of rats, snakes, and lizards. She had learned to enjoy damper and tea. The widow had noticed, also, the respect paid by the Europeans to women and wanted her child to continue to enjoy such privileges. Mitchell took Ballandella back to Sydney and brought her up with his own children.

As Mitchell's party turned for home, they stopped at Portland Bay, a few miles east of Discovery Bay. The sight that greeted them was unmistakably English. Instead of native encampments on the shore, they saw potato and turnip plots, sheep, and cattle. It was a settlement of whalers who had come two years earlier. Farther on,

John Batman negotiating with the Aborigines for the land on which Melbourne and Geelong now stand. This was the first time a colonist had not simply grabbed land in Australia. The price paid was "20 pairs of blankets, 30 knives, 12 tomahawks, 10 looking glasses, 12 pairs of scissors, 50 handkerchiefs, 12 red shirts, 4 suits of clothes, and 50 pounds of flour."

Mitchell looked down from the height of Mount Macedon and again saw English tents and vessels in Port Phillip harbor. Mitchell was not the first to have found these fertile plains. Unknown to the government in New South Wales, pioneers had come north across the waters from the long-established settlements in Van Diemen's Land.

Governor Phillip had claimed Van Diemen's Land in 1788 and Governor King sent a party in 1803 which founded a settlement at Risdon Cove on the Derwent River. Lieutenant John Bowen led the expedition of 46 men. The next year David Collins replaced Bowen and moved the settlement to the site of Hobart. After only a few months they were joined by 300 convicts. The following year, King

Left: after purchasing land from the Aborigines, Batman explored it and "about six miles up, found the river all good water and very deep. This will be the place for a village." The village, the first house of which is pictured here, was to become the present-day city of Melbourne.

sent William Paterson to settle the north coast of Van Diemen's Land at Port Dalrymple. Later Paterson moved the colony upriver to Yorktown, and renamed it Launceston.

By 1834, the settlers on the island had heard much from the whalers and the seal traders of the rich country on the southern mainland. Edward Henty, a son of an immigrant from Sussex, sailed over and established a farm at Portland. It was Henty's property that Mitchell stumbled on in 1836.

In 1835, John Batman, another settler from Van Diemen's Land, sailed across to settle the Port Phillip district. Very formally—but at an advantageous price—he purchased land on the sites of Melbourne and Geelong from the Aboriginal chiefs. The documents, weighted with such legalistic prose as "we, our heirs and successors, give, grant, enfeoff and confirm unto the said John Batman . . ." must have been meaningless to the chiefs signing them. Still, it was the first time the colonists had not simply grabbed the land from its legitimate owners. After his purchase, Batman explored. "About six miles up, found the river all good water and very deep. This will be the place for a village," he wrote of the future site of Melbourne. It was Batman's property on the Yarra that Mitchell saw from Mount Macedon and described on his return.

The rapid settlement of South Australia was due largely to the efforts of an Englishman named Edward Gibbon Wakefield. He argued that the rich lands must be sold at a price sufficient to force the settlers to remain for several years before they would actually own the property. In 1834, Wakefield's followers set up the South Australian Company. The first official settlers were landed on Kangaroo Island in 1836. Shortly after, they moved to the mainland and the city of Adelaide was founded.

Thus, within six years of Sturt's pioneering journey, South Australia was settled. No longer were the British colonists confined to the small stretch of land around Sydney.

Left: when Adelaide was founded in 1836 the settlers lived in tents gathered in a small forest clearing.

Below: by 1860 Adelaide had grown into a town with wooden houses and wide streets. The town was typical of many settlements springing up along the south coast and quickly growing into busy towns, as more and more people emigrated to the new land.

Polynesian islanders presenting Captain
Cook with a roast pig. When Cook
reached New Zealand he was struck
by the existence there of many
Polynesian customs. What he did not
know was that the Maoris had first come
to New Zealand from Polynesia.

New Zealand
6

Thousands of miles of open sea surround New Zealand. There are no clusters of nearby islands to make leapfrogging easy. The first voyages to this country were lengthy, dangerous, and determined. And they were made *en masse* by a Polynesian people at a time when no European sailor dared venture far from sight of land. Many of the Polynesian voyages were planned as colonizing expeditions, though some of their discoveries were probably accidental. The Polynesians made the perilous journey from the islands in the north in huge ocean-going canoes. One such craft carried 60 or more men with full provisions (breadfruit, sweet potato, pandanus—the edible fruit of the screw pine—fruit, dried fish, and livestock) for a long sea voyage. Fireplaces built on sand served to cook the food. Huge gourds carried fresh water. If colonization was intended, stores of seeds and roots were also packed into the canoes.

Legend has it that the great navigator Kupe was the first Polynesian to reach New Zealand in about A.D. 950. Certainly scientific dating methods have suggested that there was Polynesian settlement there by A.D. 1000. Kupe, however, is an unauthenticated tradition, as are the sailing directions he is said to have given: "Let the course be to the right hand of the setting sun, moon or Venus in the month of February." But whoever was first, there seems to have been substantial migration in the 1300's. According to Maori tradition, huge fleets from *Hawaiki* (probably Tahiti) arrived in New Zealand bringing the second great wave of Polynesians.

In 1642, Tasman sighted New Zealand—the first European to do so. Over a century later, Cook became the first to land on its shores. But after Cook's voyages, European interest in the small island group diminished. With the settlement of Sydney by the British, New Zealand again attracted European visitors. Pioneer traders began to develop the indigenous timber and flax on New Zealand's North Island for manufacture by the Australian convicts. In 1793, the *Daedalus* brought two Maori chiefs from New Zealand to teach their complex weaving skills to the prisoners. The chiefs knew little about flax, because among the Maori's weaving was done exclusively by the women but their tales of New Zealand were eagerly listened to by the Australian colonists. By the early 1800's, a real trade in flax and timber had been established.

Others visited New Zealand during these early days. From 1792, Dusky Sound, on New Zealand's South Island, was a haven for

Above: whales were plentiful along
the coast of New Zealand's North
Island, and the whalers founded many
settlements along the coast.

Above: Whale Island is one of several
small islands in the Bay of Islands,
North Island. It became a center for
whalers from all over the world,
who went there to rest and replenish
supplies and water.

sealers who hunted off the coast of Otago, New Zealand's south-western province. In 1803 and 1804, O. F. Smith discovered the Foveaux Strait "between the Southern and Southernmost Islands of New Zealand." In 1809, William Stewart charted the coast of the southernmost island now named for him. Later that same year, Captain Chase sailed north along the eastern coast and discovered that "Banks Island" was a peninsula, and not separated from the mainland as Cook had charted it.

In the North Island, whaling and trading vessels used the Bay of Islands as a base for watering and refitting. The Maoris supplied them with food and manpower in exchange for the much sought after European guns and powder. The young Maori warriors were excellent seamen and were often recruited to work on whaling vessels.

Gradually Maori men became a familiar sight in the Sydney area. Some, like Tuatara and Te Pahi, were important chiefs from the Bay of Islands area. Their presence aroused the interest of Samuel Marsden, chaplain to the colony of New South Wales. Marsden wanted to go to New Zealand to spread Christianity in that savage country. But before he could put his plans into effect, news of the *Boyd* massacre reached Sydney.

In 1809, an English vessel, the *Boyd,* called at Whangaroa Harbour to pick up a shipment of timber. On the voyage from Sydney, a young Maori on board had been cruelly treated, and when the ship anchored he invited his fellow tribesmen to exact a bitter revenge. The captain and his party were invited ashore to select their timber. The Maoris led them stealthily deep into the forest, and there proceeded to murder the entire crew. Dressed in the officer's clothing, the warriors returned to the *Boyd* and proceeded to slay all those on

Right: Maoris believed in the saying,
"an eye for an eye," so that when a
native complained of harsh treatment
while sailing on the *Boyd* they felt
it was only right that they should
massacre the crew. By the same token
they were not surprised when whalers
sought revenge and killed Maori men,
women, and children in the native pa.

board. Only a woman and her infant child, and a young cabin boy were spared. More than 70 people lost their lives in the incident. A whaling vessel in the vicinity heard of the massacre and avenged the slaughtered Europeans by razing the Maori pa and killing every man, woman, and child that could be found. Among the dead was the influential Te Pahi, who had supported Marsden's mission.

In this grim atmosphere of hate, Marsden continued with his plans to establish a New Zealand mission. But he had to wait a number of years before a ship would sail over to the islands. Finally, on November 18, 1814, Marsden set out from Sydney. With his party were two Maori chiefs, Ruatara and Hongi, under whose protection the new mission was to be founded. They arrived at the Bay of Islands in time for Marsden to preach his first sermon on Christmas Day.

Marsden had been instructed to explore as well as preach, and although he returned to Sydney soon after founding his mission, on future journeys to New Zealand he made several overland trips into the interior of North Island. On one journey he walked from Waitemata Harbour on the east coast to the Bay of Islands mission in the west, covering about 400 miles of previously unmapped country and witnessing fearful scenes of cannibalism and struggles between the Maori tribes.

Marsden was a capable man who made a great impression on the Maoris. Other dedicated missionaries followed in his footsteps. Men such as Henry Williams, William Colenso, and Thomas Chapman trekked across the North Island carrying their religion to remote Maori tribes. They always traveled with their loyal Maori guides— men who knew the way, carried the supplies, and paddled the canoes. But still they faced great hardships in opening up this virgin land. They walked over miles of shingle beaches, fought their way through rain forests, and forded seemingly impassable streams and rivers.

In 1831, Henry Williams and Thomas Chapman traveled inland to visit the Maori pa at Lake Rotorua, where they bathed in the hot mineral springs. In 1839, William Williams, Henry's brother,

walked from Port Nicholson, on Cook Strait, to Tauranga Harbour in the Bay of Plenty. His route took him along the coast to Otaki and then across the middle of the North Island. William Colenso explored the remote forested mountains of the Urewera and the Hawkes Bay area and, in 1847, visited Lake Taupo in the very center of the North Island.

By 1839, the missionaries had advanced to the most remote parts of the North Island. Without their painstaking work among the savage Maori tribes, the establishment of the first European settlement in New Zealand could never have taken place.

Edward Gibbon Wakefield was founder of the New Zealand Company which was devoted to the exploitation of the new country. He had played a large part in the settlement of South Australia. Now he was to apply his principles of scientific colonization to New Zealand.

Left: Marsden and other early pioneers were faced with dense bush, tangled shrubs, overgrown trees, and vivid plants, on routes never before traveled by a white man.

Right: Hongi Hika was a Maori chief who befriended Marsden and later visited London. The British gave him gifts which he sold to buy guns for his tribe. The guns were then used in wars with other Maori tribes.

Mount Egmont, a volcanic mountain with an almost perfectly shaped volcanic cone. The first European to climb it was Ernst Dieffenbach in 1839. His expedition was one of the first to be organized in New Zealand with a purely exploratory objective.

He sent his brother William to act as the company's agent. William arrived in the Cook Strait area in November, and at once purchased millions of acres of unexplored land from the Maori people.

The first attempt at anything approaching exploration was made by Ernst Dieffenbach, who came with Wakefield aboard the *Tory*. Dieffenbach, a professional naturalist, determined to climb Mount Egmont, one of New Zealand's major peaks. He had a difficult time recruiting Maori guides, as Mount Egmont was "tapu"—a sacred place—to the local tribes. After considerable persuasion, a local chief agreed to accompany him. Dieffenbach made two unsuccessful attempts to scale the mountain in early December, 1839. A third attempt, with a whaler named Heberly and two Maori guides, succeeded. The four men set out on December 19. Three days later they reached the snowline. The Maoris squatted down with their prayer books and refused to go any farther. Dieffenbach and his companion went on alone, cutting footsteps in the frozen snow. The next day they reached the summit, but a dense fog prevented their viewing the surrounding area. Dieffenbach records:

"After staying for some time in the vain hope that the clouds which enveloped us would disperse, we retraced our steps, and accomplished the descent with comparative ease. The natives expressed their joy at seeing us again, as they had already given us up as lost."

Shortly after the *Tory* carried Wakefield and Dieffenbach to New Zealand, the first settlers arrived at Port Nicholson. By April, 1840, over 1,000 Europeans had emigrated there and the city of Wellington was founded. Gradually the complicated country around the new settlement was explored.

In 1842, the Company sent Charles Kettle and Alfred Wills to search for land suitable for farming and grazing. The small party left Wellington in August, 1842. They went north and crossed the mountains through the Manawatu Gorge—a narrow gap between the Ruahine and Tararua ranges. Turning south, they skirted the eastern slopes of the Tararua Mountains and came to Lake Wairarapa, where they saw thousands of acres of uninhabited land. The journey was a remarkable achievement for the young and inexperienced leaders. News of the fertile land was eagerly received by the New Zealand Company. Settlers went out immediately and within a few years the first big sheep ranches in New Zealand were started.

Settlement of the North Island progressed rapidly, and by 1850 it was clear that the Europeans had used Maori experience and had mastered the main features of the topography.

But the South Island, larger and more mountainous, presented greater barriers to New Zealand's explorers. In 1842, the first settlers landed and founded the township of Nelson. They immediately began clamoring for fertile land. S. J. Cottrel was sent to the

Below: one Maori chief gave his young daughter to Ernst Dieffenbach in order that she could be brought up as a member of the explorer's family.

Above: the Maoris were always fierce and warlike and used almost anything as an excuse for a war. Revenge for an insult could result in the victim's village being sacked or the victim himself being killed and then eaten. Before many battles tribes performed the *Haka* or war dance (shown here) which originally served to frighten the enemy and raise the men into a battle frenzy.

southeast to look for it. Cottrel crossed the Richmond Mountain Range and reached the lush Wairau Valley. News of this fertile land was welcomed by the settlement at Nelson, and, despite the protests of the local Maori tribes, the New Zealand Company sent surveyors and settlers. In 1843, fighting broke out and in the struggle, 5 Maoris and 22 colonists were killed. This was one of the first skirmishes in the dispute over land between Maoris and white men which led to the bloody wars of 1845–1870.

Meanwhile, the New Zealand Company sent Charles Heaphy to the southeast to look for uninhabited land below Cape Foulwind. Heaphy, accompanied by Thomas Brunner and a Maori guide called Ekuhu, set out in March of 1846. The three men crossed first to Golden Bay and then went south along the coast. Frequently the rugged terrain demanded almost acrobatic feats. Carrying 75-pound packs, the men scrambled up sheer precipices using makeshift ropes. Heavy rains and fogs hindered their progress. But Ekuhu was a perfect bushman who never lost his way. The Maori was also adept at snaring the New Zealand weka, a bird closely resembling a chicken. Thanks to his skill, the three men rarely went hungry.

Right: Charles Heaphy was a London artist and surveyor who went to work for the New Zealand Company. During the bloody Maori Wars he was awarded the Victoria Cross for rescuing a wounded soldier under fire.

Above: almost all the New Zealand explorers employed Maoris as guides. Their knowledge and their ability to live off the land were invaluable. This drawing of Charles Heaphy's guide was made by Heaphy himself.

Slowly, Heaphy and his companions made their way down the coast. They passed the mouths of the Buller and Grey rivers, and went as far south as the Arahura River before rains and snows forced them to turn back to Nelson.

Perhaps the most important trip in the history of New Zealand exploration was made by Thomas Brunner. In December, 1846, he planned and embarked on an expedition which has become known simply as "The Great Journey." With two Maori guides and their wives, Brunner set out to find the immense plain in the South Island which the Maoris had assured him was "boundless to the eye where there were birds larger than geese which killed their dogs." One of his companions was the loyal veteran Ekuhu. Brunner planned to follow the Buller River to its mouth, continue south, and return home by a different route.

Left: Buller Gorge was typical of the country that Brunner and his party forced their way through. It was overgrown, wet, and yielded little game or other food for the men.

Right: Thomas Brunner was a British explorer and surveyor who crossed about 200 miles of unexplored country covered with dense undergrowth, and returned, in a total of 550 days.

At first all went well, but soon driving rains and the scarcity of food slowed the party to a crawl. Brunner attempted to eke out their supplies by living off the country as much as possible. At one point, after five days without food, Brunner consented to the killing of his dog Rover.

In July, 1847, they reached the mouth of the Grey River, where Greymouth now stands. From here Brunner went farther south to the Arahura and Hokitika rivers. At Tititira Head he twisted his ankle and was forced to return to the Grey. Ekuhu and his companions refused to go any farther in the winter season and Brunner was too sensible to attempt it alone. As a result, he spent the next three months in the vicinity of Greymouth, surveying, exploring the countryside, and recording the customs and traditions of the Maoris.

Late in January, 1848, Brunner and his Maori companions began their return trip up the Grey River. Weather conditions were again appalling. In April, Brunner's left side became paralyzed. Epiketu, the second Maori, and his wife left, but Ekuhu and his wife remained. Early in May, Brunner collapsed completely. He was close to blindness and his paralysis was spreading. His illness was aggravated by the onset of winter snows. At last the three travelers reached the shelter of a cave where Brunner could recuperate.

But fate had not yet finished with him. His journal records a final, unlucky incident. "A small basket of mine, which was hung from the roof of our rock to dry, fell down during the night on to the fire and was burnt. I lost all my sketches, several skins of birds, some curiosities, and some memoranda." It was a blow to the sick man, for the records represented over a year of pain and hardship.

Soon after this incident, however, Brunner's health improved and his paralysis eased. He was able to march strongly and purposefully. They soon overtook Epiketu and his wife, and together the five struggled forward. On June 15, after 550 days of traveling, they arrived at an outlying Nelson sheep station.

Brunner's trek was of the utmost importance in opening up the South Island to the new settlers. He penetrated the fertile Buller Valley and thoroughly explored the largely unknown western coast. He also traced the course of the South Island's two major rivers—the Grey and the Buller.

Between 1849 and 1851, Captain Stokes surveyed much of the coast of New Zealand in the Admiralty paddle-steamer H.M.S

Above: Sir George Grey was governor of South Australia before he became governor of New Zealand in 1845. He was greatly respected by the Maoris and helped to end the bloody fighting between the Maoris and the Europeans.

Left: the New Zealand temperate rain forests, called "bush" by settlers, are unique in their beauty. Large areas remain untouched because the height and ruggedness of the terrain make it impassable.

Below: another hazard that faced the explorers was the New Zealand rivers like the Rocky River. These rivers were often fast flowing and deep, and navigation was difficult because of the many rapids along the course.

Left: because the rivers were so dangerous explorers thought up many hopefully "safe" methods of crossing them. But men still drowned and with such frequency that drowning became known as the "New Zealand death."

Acheron. With him on the boat was J. W. Hamilton of the New Zealand Company who, during every stop for refitting, went ashore in the hope of becoming the first man to cross the backbone of South Island. Hamilton failed, but in 1852 E. J. Lee drove 1,800 sheep overland from Nelson across to the east coast. Lee followed the Wairau and the Awatere rivers, went over Barefell Pass to the Acheron and Clarence, and then through Jollie's Pass down to the Hanmer Plains. In 1857, Harper and Locke crossed from the east coast to the west. They went up the Hurunui River, across Harper's Pass and down the Taramakau to the sea.

A famous author, if not a famous explorer, Samuel Butler, systematically explored the river valleys of Canterbury in 1860, intent on finding a profitable sheep-run. He found—though he did not traverse—the Whitcombe Pass, the best route from Christchurch to the west coast.

But the barrier of the Southern Alps, splitting one side of South Island from the other like a high wall, was far from removed. In the south, the gold miners in the settlement of Queenstown on Lake Wakatipu became impatient with the failure of organized exploration to find a route to the west coast. One of their own number, A. J. Barrington, set out in December, 1863, to find a way through the difficult country. Without any Maori help, without the vegetation that had sustained Brunner in his worst moments, and in a climate infinitely more rigorous than any Brunner had known, Barrington explored a large section of the South Island's interior. He explored many of the rivers of Westland—the Pyke, the Red Pyke, the Gorge, the Cascade, the Barrier—and detailed all of the complicated country that lies between the Hollyford and the Haast.

But it was a journey filled with misfortune. One of his party disappeared, and was never seen again. Another, left alone for some weeks, was found "sitting on a stone by the river—a complete living

Above: one of the finest sights of South Island is Tasman Glacier. Eighteen miles long, it follows a straight course for 10 miles along the bases of Mount Cook, Mount Silberhorn, and finally Mount Tasman.

Above: Mount Cook, New Zealand's highest mountain, was first climbed in 1894 after the governor had offered aid to climbers and explorers who helped open the last frontiers of the islands. Conquering the peak was only possible after the climbers had conquered unexplored bush below.

skeleton." In a furious storm, Barrington himself became separated from his two companions. He spent 10 days entirely alone on the treacherous, windswept Alps before finally sighting his comrades' camp fire in Red Pyke Valley.

Barrington's party searched the rivers for gold until winter was so close upon them that their only way home was straight across country—some 7,000-foot-high snowfields and broken glaciers. From the foot of one glacier, they went up "a mile of pure ice, as pure as crystal," then over a steep snow slope to a crest that revealed only more snow. Going down a slope Barrington suddenly heard one of his companions sing out from behind him. "I turned round and he was coming down the snow at a fearful rate, head first on his back. He held the gun in one hand but had to let it go, when both he and the gun passed me at the rate of a swallow and did not stop until they reached a little flat about two miles down with a fall of 1,000 feet . . .

not hurt but a little frightened." They ate a rat—"the sweetest meat we ever ate." They rolled their way like schoolboys down frozen snow, sometimes breaking through the crust and disappearing into the drifts. When they got back to Queenstown their bones were showing through their skin. Barrington had found neither an easy route to the coast nor gold, and his accomplishments in penetrating the savage Olivine Mountains were ignored by the New Zealand authorities.

Slowly the whole of New Zealand was becoming known and settled. But it was not until the 1890's that the most formidable region of the South Island—lying almost immediately to the west of the Southern Alps—was to be properly explored. This region, part of the province of Westland, contains New Zealand's highest peaks— Mount Cook and Mount Tasman. It is also an area of glaciers—the Franz Josef, the Fox, and the Balfour—of steep gorges, and of almost perpendicular streams. The region was explored by Charles Douglas or "Mr. Explorer Douglas," as he was affectionately called.

Charles Douglas was born in Scotland and emigrated to New Zealand when he was still a boy. He represented another breed of explorers—the solitary bushman. Douglas spent more than 40 years following tortuous trails and living off the land. Although he frequently accepted assignments from the New Zealand Survey Department, he remained independent of any one group and was able to come and go, surveying and mapping where he chose.

In 1885, Douglas went with New Zealand's chief surveyor, to explore the Arawata River. The two men named the Williamson River and the Andy Glacier, and were the first to climb Mount Ionia. In 1891, Douglas alone made an important expedition up the Waiatoto River. During this trip he scaled the lower peak of Mount Ragan. His shoes having worn out completely, Douglas climbed the last 2,000 feet barefoot.

Douglas made no single journey of the length in time or distance of Brunner's ordeal. But the total experience of 40 years, and the unique advantage of months spent in the bush, were invaluable to

Right: New Zealand, showing the routes of explorers between Tasman in the mid-1600's and Brunner and Colenso in the mid-1800's

New Zealand's further exploration. In his lifetime, he mapped hundreds of major valleys in Westland. Douglas was a great figure, a solitary bushman who dearly loved the land he opened up. He expressed in his notebooks the true joy and justification of exploration: ". . . here I am after 30 years of wandering, crouched under a few yards of calico with the rain pouring and the wind and thunder roaring among the mountains, a homeless, friendless vagabond with a past that looks dreary and a future still more so. Still I don't regret having followed such a life and I know that even if I and thousands besides me perish miserably, the impulse which impels us to search the wild places of the Earth is good."

Above: Charles Douglas, seen here with A. P. Harper, another explorer, and Douglas' faithful dog Betsy, wrote of his lonely life exploring the unknown, "I have now been wandering about the uninhabited parts of New Zealand for over 5 and 30 years, always finding something in Nature new to me."

–––– Tasman	1	1642
––––– Cook	2a	1769–70
	2b	1772–4
	2c	1776–8
–––– Marsden	3a	1814–5
	3b	1820
	3c	1820
–––– Colenso	4a	1838
	4b	1841
	4c	1843–4
	4d	1847
–––– Williams	5	1839
–––– Brunner	6a	1843
Brunner (with Heaphy,	6b	1845
Fox & Ekuhu)		
Brunner (with Heaphy	6c	1846
& Ekuhu)		
Brunner (with Ekuhu)	6d	1846

C. Maria van Diemen

Wangaroa Harbour

BAY OF ISLANDS

Waimate

PACIFIC

OCEAN

Hokianga Harbour

Kaipara Harb.

Waitemate Harb.

Manukau Harb.

HAURAKI GULF

NORTH
ISLAND

BAY OF PLENTY

L. Rotorua

October 1774

NORTH TARANAKI
BIGHT

Wanganui

Taupo

L. Taupo

L. Waikare-
moana

POVERTY BAY

MT. EGMONT
8260

HAWKE
BAY

C. Kidnappers

SOUTH TARANAKI
BIGHT

RUAHINE RA.

Rangitiki

TASMAN

Manawatu

Manawatu
Gorge

Manawatu

TARARUA RA.

October 1773

SEA

GOLDEN
BAY

TASMAN
BAY

QUEEN
CHARLOTTE
SOUND

Nelson

Wairau

L. Wairarapa

Port Nicholson
Wellington

C. Palliser

Buller

L. Rotoiti
L. Rotoroa

C. Foulwind

COOK STRAIT

Grey

Taramakau

S O U T H E R N   A L P S

Hokitika

SOUTH
ISLAND

December 1773

Banks
Pena.

Tititira Head

MT. TASMAN
11,475
12,349
MT. COOK

November 1774

Pyke

L. Alabaster

Lake
Wakatipu
Queenstown

Waitaki

PACIFIC   OCEAN

Oreti

Clutha

FOVEAUX STR.

STEWART
ISLAND

Probing the Interior

7

While mountainous terrain, torrential rains, and numbing cold obstructed men such as Brunner and Barrington in their efforts to explore the small islands of New Zealand, Australian pioneers were facing very different obstacles. Mile upon mile of desert land, scorching temperatures, and a scarcity of drinking water challenged any man who sought the secrets of the vast Australian continent.

By 1840, most of southeast Australia was settled. Attention shifted to the large tracts of unexplored land which separated the colonies in the east and west. In the late 1820's, James Stirling had been sent to the west coast to find a new site for the settlement on Melville Island and in 1829 the city of Perth was founded a few miles up the Swan River. The settlement at Perth was part of a plan to send 10,000 emigrants from Britain to colonize Western Australia. The scheme, poorly prepared and organized, was a disaster and most of the colonists returned to England. Stirling had now been appoint-

ed governor. He and his young wife remained, determined to eke out an existence on the shores of the new country. But in 1839 they too left and by 1850 there were still fewer than 6,000 people in the small colony.

Early in 1837, the first serious exploration of the western coast took place. Captain George Grey and Lieutenant Lushington set out to explore the unknown northwest corner of Australia. Their plan was first to examine the area north of Dampier Land and then walk back down the coast to Perth. It was an impossible objective for the two inexperienced soldiers. Soon after landing at Brunswick Bay, the party was attacked by hostile Aborigines and Grey was speared in the leg. The venture was abandoned. On the return journey, however, they made one interesting discovery. In a cave in the Kimberley range, the men viewed one of the most superb examples of Aboriginal art. Painted on the walls of the cave were huge, brooding figures

The site of a bivouac of James Stirling and his exploring party, 50 miles up the Swan River, in March 1827. His settlement downstream on the site of present-day Perth was a failure and most of the colonists returned to England. Stirling and his wife stayed on until 1839 in an attempt to make a new life on the shores of the new country.

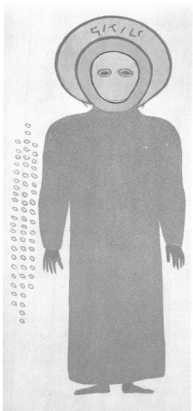

Left top: in the mid-1800's explorers were still meeting hostile Aborigines who could stop an otherwise successful expedition. But George Grey made his most exciting discovery after being wounded in a skirmish with natives.
Left below: Grey published a book describing his journeys and including drawings like this one of the cave in which he found Aboriginal paintings.
Above: a drawing discovered by Grey.

in still-bright colors. One figure was that of a man, ten-and-a-half-feet high, dressed in a scarlet robe. The face was featureless except for two staring eyes, and around his head was a halo.

Grey made another attempt to explore new territories in 1839. The journey began at Shark Bay, 420 miles north of Perth, when Grey and a small party were put ashore on Bernier Island with three small whale-boats. Grey hoped to sail down the coast making frequent forays into the coastal regions. But the Indian Ocean proved too turbulent for the small boats. One was smashed immediately after they started and the remaining two were badly battered. The men found it exhausting work rowing through the swelling seas. At one point Grey went ashore and buried all the stores in the sand to hide them from the Aborigines. But he did not allow sufficiently for high tides, and when he and his men returned to the beach they found the food completely ruined by seawater.

Three hundred miles from Perth, the two remaining boats were driven ashore and abandoned. The men, exhausted and close to starvation, began a long, desperate struggle for survival as they walked down the coast. They moved slowly, and rested frequently. Grey broke up the party while still 190 miles from Perth and made a dash for aid. Rescue parties arrived, but too late to save one 18-year-old boy, who died of hunger and exhaustion.

Efforts to link the colonies in the east and west were supported by eastern ranchers. The easterners were anxious to find a safe route to Western Australia, over which they could lead their livestock to richer pastures and better markets. In 1840, a young stockman, Edward Eyre, who had made several previous expeditions, was asked to lead an expedition west from Adelaide to Albany, a small township on the south coast. Eyre refused, declaring the route to be "quite impracticable for the transit of stock." Instead, he offered to search for a path through the interior.

Eyre left Adelaide on June 18, 1840, and spent the next three months getting nowhere in conditions near to torment. He trekked the length of Lake Torrens which was crusted with a sheet of pure white salt shining without a break across its 15- to 20-mile width. When he ventured onto the crust of salt it broke under his mount's foot, leaving horse and rider bogged in a soft black mud.

There were times when the lake was entirely hidden behind the

Scenes like this, when Eyre and his party left Adelaide, were common when explorers left for the unknown. The whole town turned out to cheer the men who were opening the continent, creating new routes and new settlements.

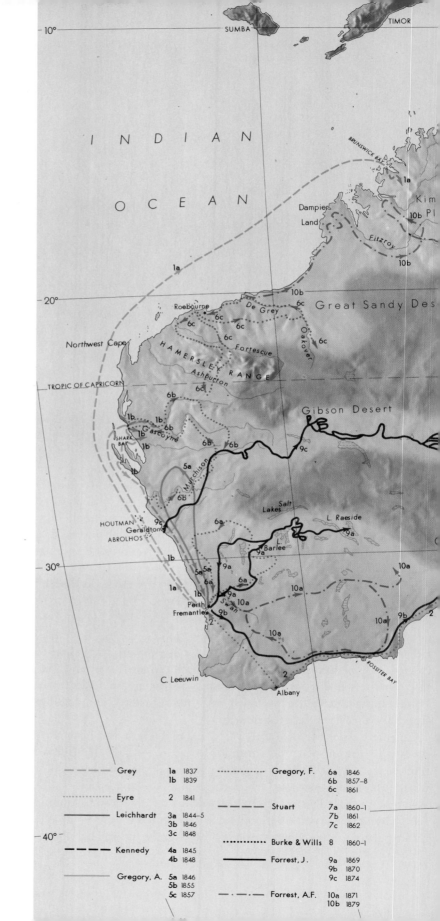

This map of the Australian continent shows the routes followed by the explorers who opened up the interior between the 1830's and 1870's.

‒ ‒ ‒ Grey	1a	1837
	1b	1839
⋯⋯⋯ Eyre	2	1841
⎯⎯ Leichhardt	3a	1844-5
	3b	1846
	3c	1848
▬ ▬ ▬ Kennedy	4a	1845
	4b	1848
⎯⎯ Gregory, A.	5a	1846
	5b	1855
	5c	1857

⋯⋯⋯ Gregory, F.	6a	1846
	6b	1857-8
	6c	1861
‒ ‒ ‒ Stuart	7a	1860-1
	7b	1861
	7c	1862
⋯⋯⋯ Burke & Wills	8	1860-1
⎯⎯ Forrest, J.	9a	1869
	9b	1870
	9c	1874
‒·‒·‒ Forrest, A.F.	10a	1871
	10b	1879

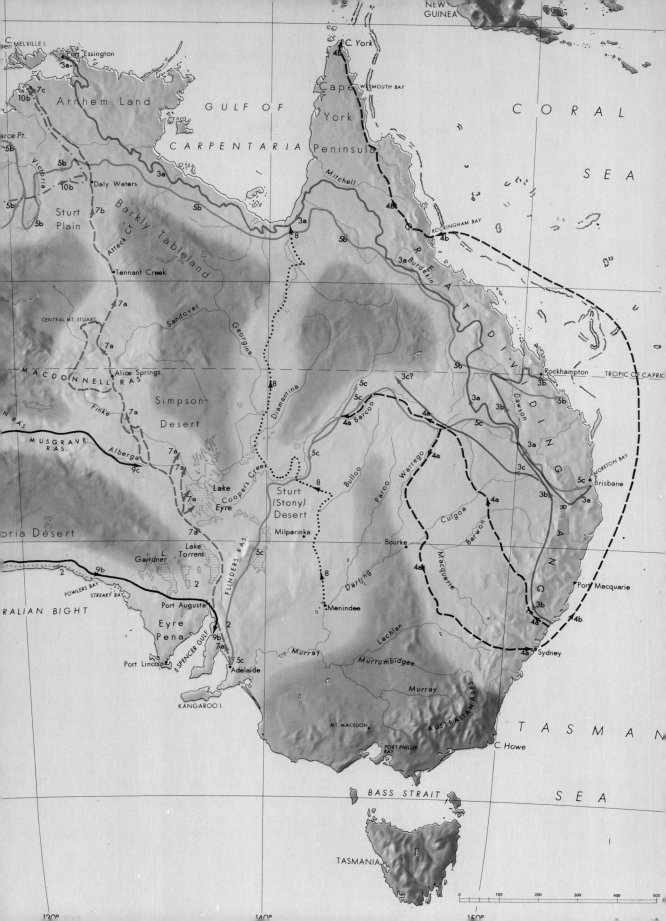

sand ridges. Twice he lost sight of it and falsely assumed it was still there, though he had in fact passed its northern end. Thus, he missed the 55-mile gap between Lake Torrens and Lake Eyre, and concluded that a great horseshoe-shaped salt lake cut off South Australia from the center. He rode six miles into Lake Eyre, until the salt crust broke suddenly and the horses sank up to their bellies. Eyre gave up and returned to Spencer Gulf.

To justify himself, Eyre determined to walk around the Bight as he had earlier been asked to do. He knew it was a useless journey, an

Lake Eyre is the lowest point on the Australian continent at 39 feet below sea level. It is one of several salt lakes or pans which have almost no water. The little rain that does fall quickly evaporates, leaving a fine crust on the 17-inch layer of salt that already covers the lake beds.

800-mile march in the hottest and driest time of the year. But he was determined to prove that it was no road for men or their cattle. He set out from Fowlers Bay on February 25, 1841, with John Baxter and three Aborigines, defying last-minute instructions from Adelaide to abandon his folly. He knew he could not hope to find any water for at least 100 miles. The temperature was 113°F in the shade. Blood-sucking flies settled on the men's arms and necks. When at last they found signs of water, they had to dig down five feet for it. One morning, with all their water gone, Eyre took a sponge and gathered a quart of dew from the grass and shrubs to make tea for breakfast.

It was a mad journey. Two of the Aborigines deserted but soon came back, desperate with hunger and thirst. After rifling the stores, they killed Baxter and fled. Wylie, the third Aborigine, remained loyal to Eyre. To assuage their hunger, they killed a horse and "jerked" the flesh. They cut it into thin strips, soaked it in the salt sea, then hung it on the bushes to dry in the sun. Sweltering by day, freezing by night, Eyre and the boy walked 148 miles in the next seven days before they reached water.

The two covered 700 miles of arid waste on foot. At Rossiter Bay the emaciated pair sighted a French whaling vessel. They lived aboard for two weeks in comparative luxury while the ship's blacksmith shoed their horses. Reprovisioned, Eyre and Wylie resumed their journey. On July 7, 1841, they walked into Albany in the southwest corner of the continent, the first men ever to arrive in the colony from the east. As Eyre had always maintained, it was no route for cattle.

Attention was now riveted on the center. The veteran Sturt declared, "I should like to put the finishing strokes to the career I

Left: Edward John Eyre, seen here arriving in Albany with Wylie, his Aborigine companion, set a new standard of endurance on his expedition. He had to dig for water and on one occasion collected dew with a sponge to provide water to make tea.

Below: few plants are hardy enough to grow in the barren desert regions of Australia. One flower Sturt and his men did find growing in the desert was afterward named Sturt's desert pea for the explorer.

began in New South Wales by unfolding the secrets of the interior and planting the ensign of my country in the centre of this mysterious region. Truly it is an object worthy to perish one's life for."

In June, 1844, with a party of 15 men, Sturt set out from Adelaide. To avoid the trap that Eyre had fallen into, Sturt went up the Murray and the Darling rivers to Menindee before turning northwest for the center.

In November, he was camped on the silver mines of Broken Hill. Unluckily, he had picked one of the hottest of summers. He and his men walked the last 150 miles to Milparinka, watching the waterholes dry up before them or having to pull out dead frogs before they could get at the last drops. Fortunately, Milparinka offered a fine supply of water. With temperatures ranging from 130° to 160°F the party was forced to camp there for the next six months.

To make life more tolerable, they dug an underground room. Still the heat was so intense that the ink evaporated from their pens, screws were drawn from boxes, and even their hair stopped growing. One man turned black and died. Winter came, bringing bitter desert cold, but it was not until July that a little rain fell.

In August, 1845, Sturt and four of his men made a dash for the

Left: Ludwig Leichhardt (1813-1848) walked 600 miles, from Sydney to Moreton Bay (Brisbane), without equipment, in 1843, only one year after first landing in Australia.

Right: explorers in camp at night. On the occasions when Aborigines were found to be hostile a lookout was kept, such as the man in the tree holding a pair of binoculars.

center. Their hopes revived when they found waterholes, fish in the creeks, and occasional game to vary their diet. But soon the spinifex (desert grasses) and the crippling sand ridges began again. The desert at first seemed to be made of tiny stones. Then came a plain, burned and cracked open by the heat of the sun. After 400 miles, Sturt turned back. He was only 150 miles from the very center of the continent, but his decision came not a moment too soon. He could not have taken his men farther and lived, for they were on the edge of the fatal Simpson Desert. During this expedition Sturt stumbled on the eastern edges of Lake Frome and Lake Blanche and confirmed that an enormous salt-lake halo, all of which he supposed to be Lake Torrens, surrounded Adelaide and separated it from the interior.

Sturt tried to reach the center again in October, this time traveling to the east of his earlier route. But this time he was stopped by the Stony Desert. At Cooper's Creek the bulb of a 127°F thermometer burst in the shade. The return journey was a fearful ordeal. The water at their forward camp gave out. They had no stores and had to wait for birds to unearth scraps that the dogs had buried. When they reached Milparinka, Sturt collapsed, blackened, scurvy-ridden, and unable to walk or ride. He was on the verge of total blindness. The party could not rest or summer would imprison them for another six months. Sturt was put on a cart and the party crawled their way back to Adelaide.

While Sturt was trapped in the interior, a half-mad German ex-

plorer, Ludwig Leichhardt, was making one of the most famous of all Australian expeditions in the northeast. Young and well-educated, Leichhardt set out to blaze a trail from Moreton Bay, the site of present-day Brisbane, to Port Essington, a garrison town in the far north near the site of Darwin. He was only 31 when he led off his ill-equipped expedition in September, 1844. Progress was monumentally slow—not surprising in view of the almost complete inexperience of the party, coupled with Leichhardt's poor discipline. In three months, the nine-man party, which included two teenagers, two Aborigines, and a volunteer convict, traveled only 450 miles. In less than a third of the projected journey, they consumed more than half their stores.

Leichhardt was a poor leader. His "navigation" was laughable. Once he calculated that his party was 20 miles out to sea. He had no experience of the bush and lost 134 pounds of flour by forcing his bullocks through such dense thickets that their packs were torn from their backs. The stores were quickly depleted and the men learned to eat anything they could lay their hands on—bandicoots (a type of small marsupial), lizards, eels, possums, snakes, dogs, even flying foxes. There was no discipline—something no leader of a party pushing its way through unknown territory could afford. One day, in a rage, Leichhardt abused one of the Aborigines who retaliated by knocking out two of the leader's teeth.

Leichhardt took his party across the Dawson River. They crossed several other rivers and watersheds before going up the beautiful,

lagoon-filled valley of the Burdekin River. They were still on the Burdekin in May, 1845, when they celebrated a number of "lasts"— they smoked their last tobacco and ate the last of the sugar, salt, and flour. But they had humor enough to name a campsite Last Damper Camp when it seemed starvation could not be far off.

Despite the presence of hostile tribes, Leichhardt neglected to keep a night watch. It was an omission that was to cost one member of the party, Gilbert, his life. The party was camped near the Mitchell River on the Cape York Peninsula. They had pitched their tents under the trees, a dangerous position in hostile territory. Suddenly from the trees above, a shower of spears rained down on the un-prepared men. The Aborigines quickly followed up with their waddies. It was some minutes before the men could get at their un-loaded guns, prime them, and frighten off the attack with a few shots. And before they did so, Gilbert had been killed and two men seriously wounded.

The party was still following the Mitchell after passing the latitude where it should have turned southwest to reach the southern coast of the Gulf of Carpentaria. Eventually Leichhardt realized his mistake and turned southwest. The men walked into Port Essington on December 17, 1845, months after they had been given up for lost. It had not been a difficult journey although it had taken them 15 months, and during it they had discovered much valuable pasture land. In this sense, Leichhardt's expedition could be said to have

Left: Port Essington near Darwin in northern Australia was founded to safeguard British interests against the threat of the French. Manned by convicts, the settlements also served as a base for parties of explorers.

Left: the Queensland "bush" is dense rain forest, with intertwining undergrowth and swiftly-flowing streams. It was through this kind of country that Leichhardt and other explorers pushed their way into the unknown.

Above: Charly and Harry were two Aborigines who acted as guides for Leichhardt and his party. The natives became increasingly dependent on the white man and welcomed any chance to live and work with pioneers.

been one of the most successful expeditions ever made in the Australian continent.

In 1847 Leichhardt set out again from just north of Sydney, intent on an even more ambitious journey. He was determined to walk around three sides of the continent—up through Queensland, across the north, and then down to Perth. Seven months later, he was no farther north than Rockhampton on the Tropic of Capricorn. His men were all down with fever. Quarreling among the men was so fierce that it was thought best to abandon the expedition.

Leichhardt regrettably lacked the respect for the Aborigines that had distinguished earlier explorers such as Flinders, Sturt, Mitchell, Eyre, and Grey. These leaders had always been careful to impress on their men that to the Aborigines the Europeans were invaders. However well the settlers might behave, they were, in the last resort, dispossessing the original inhabitants. At all times, earlier expeditions were ordered to respect and understand the Aborigine's different laws and customs, their reasoning, even their notion of revenge. Leichhardt, on the other hand, contemptuously referred to the Aborigines as "the sable gentlemen" and dismissed them as

The Australian interior proved so arid and harsh that even this offer of £2,000 ($4,800) for the first south-to-north crossing was of interest to only two men.

John Stuart led a party in the race to be first to travel from the south coast to the north. Toward the end he wrote, "I did not inform any of the party . . .that I was so near to the sea, as I wished to give them a surprise . . .Thring who rode in advance of me called out, The Sea! which took them all by surprise, and they were so astonished that he had to repeat his call before they fully understood what was meant. . . ."

cowards. It seems likely, however, that he died at their hands. In 1848, with a seven-man expedition including two Aborigines, he set out to cross the center from the east to the west and he was never seen again.

Three years later, in 1851, there began a series of expeditions expressly to look for Leichhardt and his men. The delay was understandable, for it had been assumed that it would take Leichhardt at least two years to cross the continent. Hevenden Hely led the first search party. Hely came back convinced that Leichhardt and his men had been massacred.

In 1855, a party under Augustus Gregory set out from a point near the present site of Darwin. They reached the source of the Victoria River in the Northern Territory, then continued inland for 300 miles before turning east, toward Queensland. They emerged on the eastern coast near Rockhampton. In 1857, Gregory made a second journey, searching for Leichhardt in Queensland and New South Wales. He followed the Barcoo River, where he came across a tree with an "L" carved into the bark.

Duncan MacIntyre explored the Leichhardt River that flows into the Gulf of Carpentaria, and intriguingly reported seeing children with light blue eyes, red hair, and almost white bodies among the Aborigine tribes. John Forrest trekked northeast from Perth into the Great Victoria Desert, walking, without knowing it, over rich goldfields.

Another expedition in the northeast ended tragically. In 1848, Edmund Kennedy was given the task of surveying the eastern coast of Cape York by Sydney businessmen intent on developing a port from which to trade with the East Indies. Kennedy went by sea to Rockingham Bay. On May 21, he landed with 12 men to begin the 600-mile trek through tropical jungle to the tip of the peninsula. The party tramped through bogs and marshes with hostile Aborigines harassing them at every turn. It was one of the best-equipped expeditions in Australian history. Yet a thieving storeman, slow progress, and the rigor of the journey gradually reduced Kennedy's men to starvation. A ship that was to have reprovisioned them in Princess Charlotte Bay had sailed away by the time they appeared.

When they reached Weymouth Bay, it was clear that the party would never make Cape York. Kennedy left eight men behind with food and dashed ahead with the other four to seek aid. They had not

gone far when one of the men accidentally shot himself. The injured man was left behind with two others while Kennedy pressed on with only his native guide, Jacky Jacky, for company. The two were within sight of the sea when Aborigines attacked once again and Kennedy was speared to death. Jacky Jacky went on alone to the coast after burying Kennedy's books and papers. To escape the hunters, he waded down a creek with only his nose above water. At the shore, he hailed the waiting supply vessel, the *Ariel,* and told his astonishing tale. The captain set sail immediately to look for the three men who had been left behind. They found only the most obvious signs that the men had been murdered. On they went to Weymouth Bay where the surviving men signaled frantically. But the *Ariel* did not see their fires and sailed away the next day, convinced that all were dead. When a ship did arrive, two emaciated men were staging a last stand

against the attacking Aborigines. The other six had died—"they did not suffer but withered away without pain or struggle" reported one of the skeletons who survived.

In 1860, the South Australian government offered £2,000 ($4,800) to the first man to cross the continent from south to north. There were two contenders—John McDouall Stuart, who had almost reached the center with Sturt in 1845, and Robert O'Hara Burke, a Melbourne police officer. Stuart was the first to set out.

With 2 other men and 13 horses, Stuart left Chambers Creek on January 1, 1861. The party traveled up the Finke River, crossed the Macdonnell Ranges, and on Sunday, April 22, reached the dead center. Stuart wrote in his diary: "Today I find from my observa-

Robert O'Hara Burke (1821-1861).

William John Wills (1834-1861).

Above: on his arrival in Adelaide after his successful south-to-north crossing of the Australian continent, John Stuart was greeted with the above spectacle. It was the funeral procession of Burke and Wills, his competitors for the reward offered by the South Australian government to the first man to make the crossing.

tions of the sun, 111° 00′ 30″, that I am now camped in the centre of Australia. I have marked a tree and planted the British flag there. There is a high mount about two and a half miles to the NNE. I wish it had been in the centre; but, on it tomorrow, I will raise a cone of stones and plant the flag there and name it 'Central Mount Sturt'." The name was later changed to "Central Mount Stuart" in honor of its discoverer.

The three men hurried on. Their thirst was overwhelming and at Tennant Creek they ignored gold to dig for the more precious water. At Attack Creek, the Aborigines massed with their boomerangs and spears and fired the bush in the faces of the explorers. Stuart wrote in his journal on June 22: "I have most reluctantly come to the conclusion to abandon the attempt to make the Gulf of Carpentaria. Situated as I now am it would be most imprudent." Supplies were low and his own health was bad. At any time the water might dry up behind them. Sick with scurvy and disappointment, he and his men returned to Adelaide.

Stuart had reached the 19th parallel on his first trip. Next year he went even farther and reached the 17th parallel before similar circumstances forced him to turn back. Finally, in July of 1862, his efforts were rewarded. He and his men reached the sea by the mouth of the Adelaide River near present-day Darwin. "I dipped my feet and washed my face and hands in the sea, as I promised the late Governor Sir Richard McDonnell I would do if I reached it." Stuart had lost the race across the continent to Burke, although he did not yet know it. But he had blazed such a trail, that within 10 years the Overland Telegraph line linking Adelaide with Darwin was laid and operating along the route he had taken.

The 2,000-mile return journey was the most difficult of all the trips Stuart had made. He was almost blind, was suffering from scurvy, and had to be carried on a stretcher. Emaciated, the 10-strong party arrived back in Adelaide the same day that the bodies of Burke and Wills carried were through the city on their way to burial in Melbourne.

Right: no expense was too great for the Burke and Wills expedition. 25 camels were bought from India, and fitted with swim-bladders as well as camel shoes. A special kind of cart that could be floated across rivers was loaded with everything from fishing lines to sun hats. So much equipment was provided that some had to be sold before the explorers could get under way.

Below: the desert was a hostile place for explorers whatever the weather. Most of the time it was dry and hot, but occasionally rain fell and because of the bad drainage turned the desert into an unending swamp.

Robert Burke had set out from Melbourne on August 20, 1860, at the head of the best-equipped expedition Australia had ever known. But Burke was not a good leader. Others of his party made appalling mistakes, but it was his impetuosity and lack of bushcraft which precipitated calamity. There was quarreling even before the party started out from the depot set up at Menindee where Burke had recruited a man named William Wright to show them a short cut to Cooper's Creek. The original second-in-command dropped out and William Wills, a surveyor, was promoted in his place.

Wright guided half the party to Cooper's Creek, 400 miles to the northwest, then went back for the others. He was so long in returning that Burke became impatient and began his dash for the north coast. It was December 16. Mounted on his gray charger, he took with him—on camelback—Wills, Charles Gray, and John King, a young former Indian Army soldier. The expedition's foreman, William Brahe, was left in charge at Cooper's Creek with orders to wait for three months or until the supplies ran out.

Burke had chosen a better route than Stuart. Much of it skirted the desert and lay on land now occupied by sheep and cattle stations. At first they made rapid progress. But then the rains came and bogged the animals in marshland. With half the stores gone, they were still struggling north.

It took eight weeks to reach the coast. Burke and Wills went ahead and found themselves, on February 9, 1861, in the estuary of the Flinders River, within the tidal influence but unable to see the sea. It would take at least another two days to cut their way through the jungle to reach the beach and it was time they could not afford. They had only five weeks' stores left and an eight-week journey to make.

On the most meager rations, they struggled back to Cooper's Creek in just under 10 weeks. Ironically, Gray, the strongest man in the group died on April 17. On the evening of April 21, the three men, weak and emaciated, crawled into the camp at Cooper's Creek. It was deserted. Brahe, his stores low, had waited six weeks longer than he had been instructed. But not having heard from Wright and the rest of the party, he had left that very morning. Wills recorded his disappointment: "Arrived the depot this evening just in time to find it deserted. A note left in the plant by Brahe communicates the pleasing information that they have started today for the Darling: their camels and horses all well and in good condition."

Next day Burke left a note in the tree at Cooper's Creek: "The return party from Carpentaria, consisting of myself, Wills and King (Gray dead) arrived here last night, and found that the depot party had only started the same day. We proceed on tomorrow slowly down the creek towards Adelaide by Mount Hopeless, and shall endeavour to follow Gregory's track; but we are very weak. The two camels are done up and we shall not be able to travel faster than four or five miles a day. Gray died on the road from exhaustion and fatigue. We have all suffered from hunger. Greatly disappointed at finding the party here gone. Robert O'Hara Burke, Leader. April 22, 1861. P.S. The camels cannot travel and we cannot walk, or we should follow the other party. We shall move very slowly down the creek."

After five days' walking they were forced to turn back for lack of water. The Aborigines were kind and gave them fish. The three men learned to find nardoo seeds and cook them to make a flour-like cake. They were camped on the creek, about 50 miles downstream

Left: Cooper's Creek only flows when there is heavy rain in its upper reaches. Then it floods a wide area and for a short time brings the "dead heart" of the continent to life.

Above: for Burke, Wills, and King, Cooper's Creek was the scene of a series of misunderstandings and near misses that resulted in the death of the two leaders.

from the depot. Brahe returned on May 8 after he met up with the laggardly Wright at last making his way from Menindee. But the camp looked exactly as he had left it. Burke, Wills, and King had been careful to obliterate all signs of their visit so that the Aborigines would not come up and destroy the note they had left behind. Brahe rode away, unaware that his comrades were near death only a few miles downstream.

The lives of the three men now depended on keeping close to the friendly Aborigines where they had camped. Wills, on his own, went back to the depot to leave another message giving their location, but he was three weeks too late. Only history was to read his note: "May 31, 1861. We have been unable to leave the creek. Both camels are dead and our provisions are done. Mr. Burke and King are down on the lower part of the creek. I am about to return to them when we shall all probably come up this way. We are trying to live the best way we can like the blacks but find it hard work. Our clothes are going to pieces fast. Send provisions and clothes as soon as possible. The depot party having left . . . have put us in this fix. I have deposited some of my journals here for fear of accidents."

Wills returned to his companions. Gradually he and Burke weakened until they were incapable of gathering nardoo or even pounding it for flour. The Aborigines who had been in the habit of giving them fish moved on. For days King looked after the other two. But when he began to show signs of weakness, it was decided that he and Burke should leave Wills with eight days' supply of nardoo, water, and firewood and go in search of the Aborigines for help. Burke managed for only two days before he collapsed. King made him a good evening meal from a crow which he had shot and some pounded nardoo. "I hope you will remain with me here till I am quite dead," Burke said. "It is a comfort to know that someone is by." He died at eight the next morning. He left a message for the Exploration Committee: "I hope we shall be done justice to. We fulfilled our task but were"—here he began to write the word "abandoned" but crossed it out and continued—"not followed up as I expected. The depot party abandoned their post."

King went back and found Wills dead also. The last entry in his diary read: "I am weaker than ever although I have a good appetite and relish the nardoo much, but it seems to give no nutriment. I may live four or five days if the weather continues warm. Starvation

As time wore on, people in Melbourne became more and more concerned about the disappearance of Burke and Wills, and the rest of their party. Several search parties went out but failed to find any sign of the expedition, and there was still speculation as to whether the explorers were dead or alive. But the questions were answered when Alfred Howitt found the bodies of Burke and Wills, and the emaciated King who had been living in an Aborigine village.

on nardoo is by no means very unpleasant but for the weakness one feels and the utter inability to move oneself."

There was nothing left for King to do but join the Aborigines. He shot crows and hawks for them, and in return they gave him nardoo and fish and provided him with shelter. After three months, a rescue party arrived under Alfred Howitt. They found King a wasted shadow, hardly to be distinguished as a human being. The bodies of the dead leaders, Burke and Wills, were carried back to Melbourne for burial.

The Challenge of the Desert

8

In 1872, the Overland Telegraph line, connecting Adelaide in the south with Darwin in the north, was opened along the trail that Stuart had blazed. No one yet knew what lay to the west of the line, and Australia's second great race began. The 1,200 miles of unknown land between the telegraph line and Perth on the west coast were first challenged by Ernest Giles. Giles was a fine bushman who was also a scholar. He read Byron at breakfast and the names he gave his discoveries—Mount Peculiar, Glen Thirsty, The Stinking Pit, Mount Unapproachable—hark back to *The Pilgrim's Progress*, John Bunyan's story of a Christian's journey through life, in which people and places represent vices and virtues.

On August 11, 1872, Giles set out from the Charlotte Waters Telegraph Station with two companions. He fully explored the area around the Macdonnell Ranges before the lack of water forced him temporarily to abandon the idea of pushing across the continent. Giles returned to Adelaide intent on recruiting a new expedition. He had seen enough to realize it was going to be one of the most difficult of journeys. But before he could set out a second time, two others, Peter Warburton and William Gosse, were off.

Peter Warburton was aged 60 when he led his party out from Alice Springs on April 15, 1873. His party consisted of his son Richard, who was a surveyor, 4 servants, and 17 camels. They carried provisions for 6 months. Unluckily, Warburton had chosen a drought year. Three camels broke down in the scorching heat. The

Left: desert scene in the western interior of Australia. Blazing heat and lack of water proved the death of many of the men who tried to explore the vast unknown lands between Perth and the Overland Telegraph line between Adelaide and Darwin.

Right: Ernest Giles (1835-1897) was an Englishman who emigrated to Australia. Between 1872 and 1876 he made four journeys into the western deserts and in 1875 made the first return trip across western Australia.

men were forced to stay at each well until they scouted a new one to move on to. Once they were unable to move for six weeks. The search for water forced them toward the northwest so that although they covered 1,000 miles in three months they were no nearer to Perth than they had been at Alice Springs.

Warburton abandoned his attempt to reach Perth and headed for the Oakover River in the northwest. He went blind in one eye and became so ill he had to be strapped to his camel. One of the men went mad. Finally, the party split up, and the stronger members went ahead for aid. The others settled down to eat the last camel, knowing there were only a few weeks between them and starvation. Aid arrived just in time. Warburton had traveled over 2,000 miles of fearful country and discovered nothing. But no one before had traveled so far across the great deserts of the northwest.

Above: in desperate need of water Giles found a stagnant and putrid water hole hidden below some scrub. Necessity forced him to use it and he called it the "Stinking Pit."

Right: at an age when most men would be content to watch younger men explore new country, in 1873, Peter Warburton set out to cross hundreds of miles of desert. He was 60 years old.

Below: Peter Warburton reasoned that camels, used to living in the desert where no steady supply of water is available, would be an ideal pack animal to use for crossing the interior of Australia.

Below: Peter Warburton reasoned that camels, used to living in the desert where no steady supply of water is available, would be an ideal pack animal to use for crossing the interior of Australia.

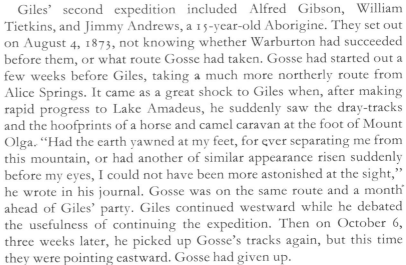

Giles' second expedition included Alfred Gibson, William Tietkins, and Jimmy Andrews, a 15-year-old Aborigine. They set out on August 4, 1873, not knowing whether Warburton had succeeded before them, or what route Gosse had taken. Gosse had started out a few weeks before Giles, taking a much more northerly route from Alice Springs. It came as a great shock to Giles when, after making rapid progress to Lake Amadeus, he suddenly saw the dray-tracks and the hoofprints of a horse and camel caravan at the foot of Mount Olga. "Had the earth yawned at my feet, for ever separating me from this mountain, or had another of similar appearance risen suddenly before my eyes, I could not have been more astonished at the sight," he wrote in his journal. Gosse was on the same route and a month ahead of Giles' party. Giles continued westward while he debated the usefulness of continuing the expedition. Then on October 6, three weeks later, he picked up Gosse's tracks again, but this time they were pointing eastward. Gosse had given up.

Gosse, however, has his place in Australian history. He was the first European to see Ayers Rock, the great monolith 275 miles southwest of Alice Springs. The rock is a 1,100-foot-high piece of sandstone 5 miles in circumference, rising sheer from the sand and the porcupine grass. It can be seen from 150 miles away, a low purple mound above the horizon. At close sight the rock is overwhelming,

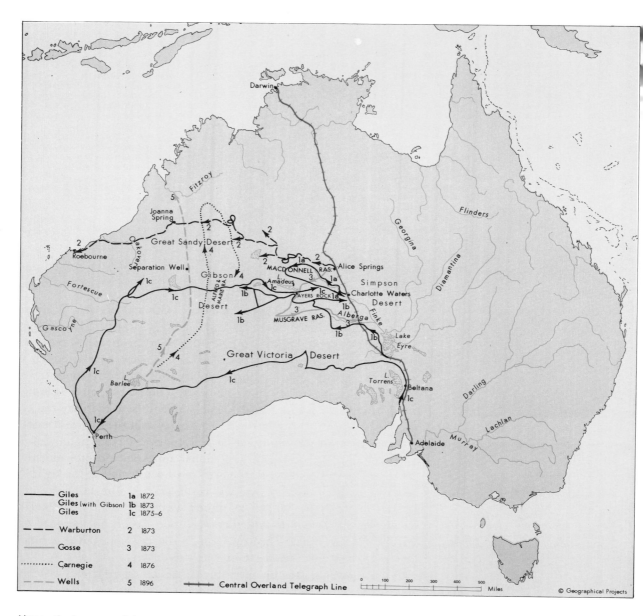

Above: the journeys of the
explorers of the 1870's and 1890's
as they crossed the vast, barren
deserts of Western Australia.

changing color as the sun moves over it, appearing sometimes red, sometimes brown, sometimes almost black.

Elated now that Gosse had retired, Giles pressed on. But, as the land became more and more arid, progress became increasingly difficult. He established a base camp at Fort Mueller, and made innumerable sorties from it without once breaking through. On Christmas Day, 1873, the four men were sitting down to a dinner of wallaby steak, pumpkin, melted butter, and rum when Aborigines suddenly attacked them in force. "The more prominent throng were led by an ancient individual who, having fitted a spear," wrote Giles, "was just in the act of throwing it down among us, when Gibson seized a rifle and presented him with a conical Christmas box, which smote the rocks with such force and in such near proximity to his hinder parts that in a great measure it checked his fiery ardour and induced most of his more timorous following to climb with most

Ayers Rock is a giant outcrop of rock in the Northern Territory of Australia forming the largest monolith in the world. The first European to see Ayers Rock was William Gosse during his unsuccessful attempt to cross the western deserts of Australia. Gosse named the rock after Sir Henry Ayers, premier of South Australia.

Ayers Rock, 275 miles southwest of Alice Springs, is remarkable for the way it changes color in different light. It contains several networks of caves. The Aborigines found these caves before the white man and decorated them with paintings. The colors used were mainly red, yellow, black, white, and brown. The paint was applied to cave walls with twigs, feathers, or just fingers. The meanings of the symbols are still a mystery but it is thought they are connected with religious theory and ritual.

perturbed activity over the rocks. The ancient more slowly followed and then from behind the fastness of his rocky shield, he spoke spears and boomerangs to us, though he used none."

In the new year the party continued their efforts to break through to the west. In April, Giles decided to make one last attempt, after first ensuring that he would have an easy retreat afterward along the Petermann Range to Mount Olga and the Musgraves. He planned to take Tietkins with him, as he had done on most sorties. But Gibson complained bitterly of being left behind at base, and so Tietkins relinquished his place to him.

The two men set off on April 20 with a week's supplies and four horses. They intended to cache some of the food and water and pick it up on the return journey. At the same point, they would turn two horses loose to make their own way back to camp.

After three days journeying they came in sight of the Alfred and Marie ranges. Perhaps on the other side lay success. But suddenly Gibson's horse collapsed and died. They had already cached their

Above: the Christmas Day attack on Giles and his party was led by an old man who shouted abuse at the explorers. In an attempt to translate his remarks Giles wrote, "... he undoubtedly stigmatised us as a vile and useless set of lazy, crawling, whitefaced brutes ... being too lazy to walk like black men....."

Right: in an attempt to reach help, Gibson rode back to base taking a compass to keep him on the track. Giles later wrote, "I knew he didn't understand anything about compasses, as I had often tried to explain them..." and in fact Gibson disappeared into the desert and was never seen again.

stores and sent the other two horses home. They were 110 miles from base, 90 miles from the last water hole, and 30 miles from where they had left a little food and some kegs of water. With little water left and only one horse there was no alternative but to turn back. For a short while they took turns riding the single mount but Giles soon realized that their rate of progress was too slow. He put Gibson on the horse, told him to take some of the food and water, and ride back to base for help.

Gibson rode off and Giles began his long walk. At the cache he picked up the remaining water—two gallons to be made to last at least six days—and a few thin sticks of dried meat. The only economical way to carry the water was to leave it in the keg, rather than transfer it to his waterbag which would soak up much of the valuable liquid. The keg weighed 15 pounds, the water another 20 pounds. With the rest of his equipment, Giles now carried a load of 50 pounds. "After I had thoroughly digested all points of my situation," he wrote, "I concluded that if I did not help myself, Providence would not help me. I started, bent double by the keg, and could only travel so slowly that I thought it scarcely worth while to travel at all. I became so thirsty at each step I took that I longed to drink up every drop of water I had in the keg, but it was the elixir of death I was

Explorers often saw mirages, like the
shimmering haze in the top of this
photograph, suggesting much-sought-
after water which receded or disappeared as the explorers approached.

burdened with, and to drink it was to die, so I restrained myself. By next morning I had only got about three miles, and to do that I travelled mostly in the moonlight. The next few days I can only pass over as they seemed to pass with me, for I was quite unconscious half the time, and I only got over about five miles a day."

Then to his horror, Giles saw that the two loose horses had swerved off the tracks leading back to base and Gibson had followed them. Near to death himself under the scorching sun, Giles could only assume that Gibson would eventually have realized his error and returned to the proper track farther on. Giles plodded on, his head made light with hunger and thirst. The sun beat down on him remorselessly. Often he lost consciousness and could not tell what day it was or where he was. He lay in the shade by day and marched by night. Usually when he found a desert oak to lie under there would be a huge bulldog ants' nest underneath it, denying him its shade. When he walked his path was through thick bushes. "My arms, legs, thighs, both before and behind, were so punctured with spines, it was agony only to exist," he recorded. "The slightest movement and in went more spines. They broke off in the clothes and flesh, causing the whole of the body that was punctured to gather into minute pustules which were continually growing and bursting. My clothes, especially inside my trousers, were a perfect mass of prickly points."

Twenty miles from the water hole, Giles drank the last of his water. At least the unloading of the keg from his back increased his pace. He had not eaten for five days and would faint from time to time, but he reached the water hole and began to drink his fill. A

153

John Forrest leading his men across the vast desert that cut Western Australia off from the rest of the continent. Although the interior of Australia is called "desert" it is not desert in the sense of miles of sand dunes. A little rain falls each year and when it does, coarse grasses, in particular spinifex, shown here and opposite, and shrubs grow, only to dry up slowly and die after the rain.

wallaby passed close by him and dropped its baby from its pouch. Giles grabbed it. "The instant I saw it, like an eagle I pounced on it and ate it raw, dying as it was, fur, skin and all. The delicious taste of that creature I shall never forget. I only wished its mother and father to serve in the same way."

That night he completed the remaining 20 miles to camp. It was dawn when he shook Tietkins awake and asked after Gibson. But Tietkins had seen neither Gibson nor the two loose horses. Next day, despite his appallingly weak condition, Giles set out with Tietkins to look for their comrade. He was not to be found. He had ridden away to nowhere, to die slowly in the burning desert. Giles called it the Gibson Desert in memory of its first known white victim. The party returned to Charlotte Waters to find that John Forrest had made the inland crossing from west to east.

John Forrest, like Hume, was an Australian by birth and upbringing. He began exploring in the west at the age of 22, looking for the spot where the Aborigines said Leichhardt had died. He went over gold country, northeast from Perth, past Lake Barlee, as far as Mount Weld. In 1870, he traced Eyre's route along the Great Australian Bight, from Perth to the Spencer Gulf about 100 miles north of Adelaide.

Forrest was eager to challenge the unconquered west—"a great lone land, a wilderness interspersed with salt marshes and lakes,

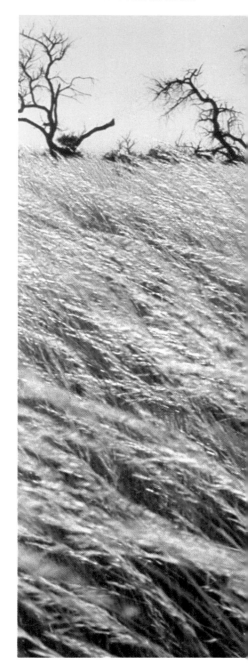

One of the few things to grow in the Australian desert is spinifex, a coarse, spiny grass. Experts believe that there is water under the desert and if it could be brought to the surface the land could become fertile.

barren hills and spinifex deserts." He was persuaded to wait, however, until both Giles and Gosse had failed in their attempts to make the east-west crossing. The governor of Western Australia, Weld, was anxious that Forrest's expedition should not appear to be in jealous competition with the eastern states. Finally, on April 1, 1874, Forrest left Geraldton, on the coast facing Houtman Abrolhos. After six months' steady traveling he and his men reached the Peake River by Lake Eyre on the Overland Telegraph line.

Inevitably his men had suffered in the desert, but Forrest was a superb leader, and had planned the expedition carefully. Forrest would scout ahead for water and the men followed only when they were certain of a fresh supply. They had been able to vary their diet with rats and emu eggs. Only once had they been attacked by the Aborigines.

It had been a wonderfully successful expedition, under the leadership of a courageous man. Pierre, one of the Aborigines, gave tribute to his leader on their return to Perth: "Many a time I go into camp in the morning, going through desert places, and swear and curse and say, 'Master, where the deuce are you going to take us?' I say to him 'I'll give you a pound to take us back!' Master say, 'Hush! What are you talking about? I will take you all right through to Adelaide.' And I always obey him. Gentlemen, I am thankful that I am in the Town Hall. That's all I got to say."

Forrest's was the last major exploration of Australian territory. But there were still many ends to be tied up. Giles needed recompense for his failures and received it in 1876 when he became the first man to make the return trip east to west. He set out from Beltana on the Overland Telegraph line on May 6, 1875, this time with camels. The party took a southerly latitude, trekking across the Great Victoria Desert in murderous conditions. Giles came close to being killed when a group of treacherous Aborigines attacked at Ularring. The inhabitants had been so friendly that they had been allowed to stay in the party's camp for a few days. Especially welcome was a little girl of 10 who became a great favorite with the men. But at dinner time on the third evening of their stay, the Aborigines in the camp gave a signal to their hidden comrades and when the explorers looked up, they saw over a hundred men advancing on them, armed to the teeth in full battle array. Giles was seized by the throat to prevent him firing his rifle but the others reacted quickly

Crossing the Great Victoria Desert Giles wrote in his journal: "We had come 323 miles without having seen a drop of water.... There was nothing that the camels could eat.... Before us, and all along the western horizon, we had a black-looking and scrubby rise of very high sandhills...."

and routed the attackers before they were near enough to throw their spears. It was then that Giles remembered some signs that the little girl had made to him in the afternoon. She had been trying to give him warning of the impending attack, but he had failed to understand.

On his return journey, Giles could not resist the challenge of the Gibson Desert. In violent extremes of heat and cold (100°F by day, 15°F by night, and in windstorms that were "hell on earth," Giles crossed the terrain that had taken away his comrade two years earlier. While the party rested, he went out alone to search for traces of Gibson. But he found nothing. Giles had to be led much of the way home as blindness intermittently attacked his eyes and the ever-present flies busied themselves on the inviting inflammations. Giles arrived at the Peake River on August 23, 1876, having at last won his place among the dozen most important Australian explorers. But his achievements received no recognition. He died in 1897, while working in the Inspector of Mines Office in Coolgardie.

Coolgardie was but one of the many places Giles had put on the map in his younger days.

In 1879, Alexander Forrest, John Forrest's brother, made a trip across the north of the continent from the De Grey River in the northwest, up to the Kimberley Mountains, and across to the Overland Telegraph line. The last stage of his journey took on a nightmare quality as he and another man dashed ahead for aid to help his stricken party. His younger brother had gone insane and two others had collapsed. Forrest's party had been looking for land for western Australian expansion. Although he failed to penetrate the Kimberley Mountains, Forrest found 20 million acres of well-watered pastureland for the government.

In 1891, in the worst drought in memory, David Lindsay traveled diagonally across the South Australian deserts, mapping 80,000 square miles of unknown territory while occasionally digging 15 feet down into the sand for water. In 1896, Lawrence Wells and David Carnegie both made south-north crossings of the Western

Anthony Trollope, a British novelist, visited Australia in 1871, and wrote of bushmen, seen here gathering at a general store: "They come and go. . . . They probably have their wives elsewhere, and return to them for a season. They are rough to look at, dirty in appearance, shaggy, with long hair, men who, when they are in the bush, live in huts, and hardly know what a bed is. But they work hard, and are both honest and civil. Theft among them is almost unknown."

Australian deserts. Wells lost two men who died from thirst. Carnegie found a new way of discovering water. He would capture an Aborigine, feed him salt beef, and then follow him as he went to quench his thirst. This is Empty Australia—no rivers, no hope of pastoral possibilities. An American geologist went there in 1924 and found insurmountable sand ridges. The Australian desert may not be the traditional carpet of sand—in most places it is covered by scrub and bush—but there is no better word to describe it.

One part of Australia remained unconquered until 1936—the terrible Simpson Desert that lies to the north of Lake Eyre. Many men died in it as the stockmen edged toward its fringe and took risks traveling from one station to another. Cecil Madigan flew over it in 1929 and described it as "a pink and gigantic circular gridiron ribbed with close straight sand ridges from horizon to horizon." It was Madigan who gave the desert its name and declared that it could never be crossed. But a farmer named Edmund Colson who lived on the western edge of the desert insisted it could be done. He had to wait through seven years of drought before he could test his plan. The moment the first rain fell in 1936, Colson recruited an Aborigine boy called Peter, saddled five camels, and loaded them with water and tinned food to last a month.

Colson's theory was that the rain would now germinate the millions of seeds that had been lying dried and preserved in the sand for many years. The seeds would be like a form of instant plant, and would provide all the food and moisture his camels would need. Freezing at night, sweltering by day, Colson and Peter began the crossing. Sometimes the tops of the ridges were so deep in loose sand that the camels had to crawl their way over them. On the third day Colson's theory was miraculously proved right. He and Peter had climbed yet another giant ridge and there below them was an oasis of green grass. A purple carpet, the flower of the parakelia, lay welcoming over the sand. The leaves of the plant oozed with moisture. Colson and Peter knew they had succeeded. Between each line of ridges, the desert had sprung to life. Soon they saw animals, a rabbit, a fox, a kangaroo, a dingo, all attracted to these sudden and momentary Edens. After 16 days they rode into Birdsville, to be greeted only with disbelief—until they could develop their photographs and prove their amazing story.

Australia was conquered. It was less than 150 years since the

Right: South Australia, showing the routes of the three explorers—Eyre, Warburton, and Stuart—who opened the interior in the middle 1800's

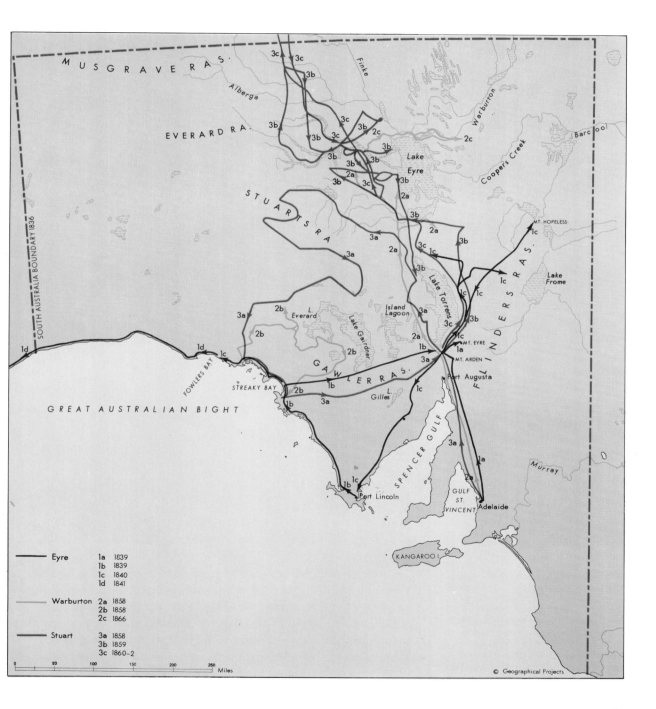

M U S G R A V E R A S.

EVERARD R A.

Alberga

Finke

Warburton

(Bar oo)

3c 3c
3b
3b
2c
2c
3c
3b
3b 3c
3b 2c
3b 3b 3b
2a
3b
3b 3c 3b
2a

Lake
Eyre

Coopers Creek

SOUTH AUSTRALIA BOUNDARY 1836

S
T
U
A
R
T
S
R
A.

3a

3a

2a

2a
3b
3c
1c

MT. HOPELESS

1c

Lake
Frome

3a

2b
L.
Everard

3a

2b

Lake Gairdner

Island
Lagoon

2b

Lake Torrens

1c
1c
1c
3b
3c
1c

MT. EYRE

F
L
I
N
D
E
R
S
R
A
S.

1d

1d

1c

Fowlers Bay

STREAKY BAY

2b

1b

2b
3a

G A W L E R R A S.
L.
Gilles

3a
2a
1b
1a
3a

1c

MT. ARDEN

Port Augusta

1c

G R E A T A U S T R A L I A N B I G H T

1b
1c

Port Lincoln

S
P
E
N
C
E
R

G
U
L
F

3a
1a

Murray

2c
GULF
ST.
VINCENT

Adelaide

KANGAROO I.

	Eyre	1a	1839
		1b	1839
		1c	1840
		1d	1841
	Warburton	2a	1858
		2b	1858
		2c	1866
	Stuart	3a	1858
		3b	1859
		3c	1860-2

0   50   100   150   200   250
Miles

© Geographical Projects

Above: Aborigines in Arnhem Land take part in a *corroboree,* a traditional Aborigine festival. Although there was no full-scale war between Aborigine and white man during the conquest of Australia, the opening up of the continent and the introduction of a western way of life altered the Aborigines' world beyond recognition.

first settlers had arrived. It had been a remarkably peaceful story, a natural spread of a pastoral people occupying new lands in the wake of some of the most hardy and courageous explorers the world has known. The history of the country's development is perhaps most astonishing in the total absence from it of war, either against the Aborigines or between the Europeans themselves. The battles had all been with the mysterious and powerful continent.

Left: in the early 1600's, Dutch ships like those pictured here, discovered the western coast of Australia.

Appendix

Australia and New Zealand were once part of the vague southern land mass called *Terra Australis Incognita*. Today these countries have been given the name *Lands of the Southern Cross*. (The Southern Cross is the constellation or group of stars in the shape of a cross which is visible in the Southern Hemisphere.) The triumph over the unknown was made possible by the courageous and determined explorers who, by their efforts, opened up Australia and New Zealand.

Dominating and enriching the story of the discovery and exploration of the lands of the Southern Cross are the personal accounts of the men involved. Many of these accounts, written under the most difficult conditions, convey the flavor and excitement of discovery as no other writing can.

Wherever possible, this book has attempted to incorporate firsthand accounts in the text itself. Additional documents of importance or of narrative interest are included in the following supplement. It is hoped that these documents—drawn from a variety of sources—will add to the scope and to the enjoyment of the book as a whole.

To facilitate reference to individual explorers mentioned in the text, an alphabetical list of explorers is included in the supplement. A short biography is given for each explorer, together with route maps of some of their journeys.

The supplement concludes with a glossary, index, and picture credits. The glossary contains a fuller explanation of important terms and concepts, as well as brief definitions of unfamiliar words.

Tasman's Instructions

In August, 1642, Abel Tasman embarked on his first voyage of discovery. His instructions from the Dutch East India Company stressed the commercial intent of the voyage; admonished Tasman to deal fairly with the inhabitants of unknown lands; and gave explicit advice on the crew's diet.

"If, unlikely as it may be, you should happen to come to any country peopled by civilized men, you will give to them greater attention than to wild barbarians, endeavoring to come into contact and parley with its magistrates and subjects, letting them know that you have landed there for the sake of commerce, showing them specimens of the commodities which you have taken on board for the purpose, for which we refer you to the specified invoice; closely observing what things they set store by and are most inclined to; especially trying to find out what commodities their country yields, likewise inquiring after gold and silver whether the latter are by them held in high esteem; making them believe that you are by no means eager for precious metals, so as to leave them ignorant of the value of the same; and if they should offer you gold or silver in exchange for your articles, you will pretend to hold the same in slight regard, showing them copper, pewter, or lead and giving them an impression as if the minerals last mentioned were by us set greater value on.

Above: an illustration in Tasman's *Journal* depicting the inhabitants of the Friendly Islands in their traditional dress. In the background, native proas lie at anchor. In the right-hand corner, Dutch sailors collect water.

Left: while at anchor off the South Sea Islands, Tasman's ships were often surrounded by native proas whose friendly occupants were anxious to trade with Dutch sailors.

"You will prudently prevent all manner of insolence and all arbitrary action on the part of our men against the nations discovered, and take due care that no injury be done them in their houses, gardens, vessels, or their property, their wives, etc; nor shall you carry off any of the inhabitants from their country against their will; should, however, any of them be voluntarily disposed to accompany you, you are at full liberty to bring them hither.

"If in the course of this voyage there should be discovered any rich countries or regions, islands, or passages, profitable to the Company, we shall not be found ungrateful towards the managers of the expedition and all the well-behaved men taking part in it, duly recompensing the pains and trouble they have been at, and honoring them with such rewards as their services done shall be found to have deserved; on all which all of you may rely to the fullest extent.

Tasman's Instructions

"The ships are manned with 110 able-bodied men, to wit the *Heemskerck* with 60, and the *Zeehaen* with 50; they are victualled and provided with all necessaries for 12, and with rice for 18 calendar months; out of these you will have the ordinary rations regularly and properly served out, with two meat-days and one bacon-day every week, and one mutchkin and a half of arrack everyday; all-which you will cause to be properly arranged and seen to. Of strong arrack each of the ships will take on board two hogsheads, to be in moderation served out in cold weather for the sake of the men's health. But above all you will carefully husband the fresh water, that you may not come to be in want of it, or be forced to delay your voyage in order to seek it, or return from such search un-successfully."

Journal of the Discovery of the Unknown Southland in 1642 *Abel Janszoon Tasman, trans. J. E. Heeres (Fred Muller & Company: Amsterdam, 1898) p. 135.*

Above: hostile islanders like these two warriors from Moa, one of the Indonesian Islands, often prevented the Dutch from landing and replenishing their supply of water.

Below: the islands of Moa and Insou as mapped by Tasman. The map shows Tasman's vessels—the *Heemskerck* and the *Zeehaen*—approaching the islands.

A Penal Colony in New South Wales

Transportation of English criminals to the American colonies was abruptly halted by the American War of Independence. England now faced the problem of founding a new settlement to receive convicted felons. On August 18, 1786, Lord Sydney, British Home Secretary, wrote to the Lords Commissioners of the Treasury proposing New South Wales as a penal colony.

"Whitehall, 18 August, 1786"

"My Lords,

"The several gaols and places for the confinement of felons in the kingdom being in so crowded a state that the greatest danger is to be apprehended. . . .

"I am, therefore, commanded to signify to your Lordships his Majesty's pleasure . . . for effectually disposing of convicts and rendering their transportation reciprocally beneficial both to themselves and to the State, by the establishment of a colony in New South Wales, a country which, by the fertility and salubrity of its climate connected with the remoteness of its situation (from whence it seems hardly possible for persons to return without permission) seems peculiarly adapted. . . ."

Historical Records of New South Wales, Vol. 1, Part 2—Phillip, 1783–1792 (*New South Wales Government, 1889–1901: Charles Potter, Government Printer, Sydney*) pp. 14–17.

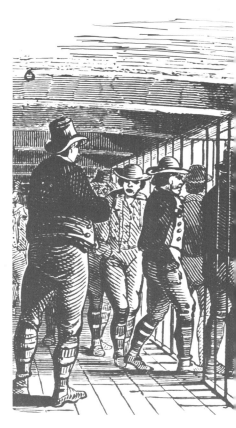

Above: convicts aboard a prison hulk moored in the River Thames. The risk of epidemics spreading from these unhealthy makeshift jails led to the establishment of a penal colony in New South Wales.

Left: prisoners attend religious services on board ship while being transported to the new colony at Sydney.

Prison Life in Early Australia

Convicts transported to Australia played a major role in the settlement of the early colonies. They built towns and roads and provided a source of cheap labor for the running of farms and sheep stations. But their lot was not an easy one. In 1838, after careful study of existing conditions, Alexander Maconchie made a report to Parliament on the abuse of prisoners in Van Diemen's Land.

"The convict, on his arrival in the colony, has no choice either of master or occupation, but is arbitrarily assigned as may be determined by a public board. . . . His master is, at the same time, rarely indulgent; he is accustomed to find his convict servants evade their work whenever possible; and he regards all excuses, therefore, with suspicion. A new comer, accordingly, like all his fellows in their day, even if he does his best, is not thought to do so . . . . The intercourse between him and his master is thus hostile almost from the beginning; and it rapidly becomes a continued series of efforts, on the one part to evade work, on the other to resist such evasion.

Above: a convict chain gang in Sydney awaits assignment. Convicts proved a valuable source of cheap labor for the growing Australian colony.

Left: an early portrayal of the town of Parramatta, a few miles north of Sydney, shows prisoners at work and at rest. A convict's life in the early colony was one of hard labor.

The ill-will which thus, on both sides, increases, is reciprocally shown by covert injury, and violent punishment and reproach. . . . The punishments adjusted to each ascertained offence are severe, even, as I think, to excessive cruelty. Besides corporal punishment to the extent of 50, 75, and even in some rare instances, 100 lashes, solitary confinement, and months, or even years, of hard labour in chains (on the roads, or at a penal settlement), are lightly ordered for crimes in themselves of no deep dye; petty thefts (chiefly in order to procure liquor), drunkenness, insolence, disobedience, desertion, quarrelling among themselves, and so forth. Yet even these punishments are ineffectual restraints. The convict is, in truth, beyond patient endurance, miserable, and the tokens of wretchedness cannot be kept under."

Thoughts on Convict Management, *Alexander Maconchie, from Convict Discipline in Van Diemen's Land (Ordered by the House of Commons to be Printed 26 April, 1838) p. 7.*

On the Murrumbidgee

In 1829–1830, Charles Sturt led an expedition to explore the rivers of southern Australia. It was one of the most important and difficult journeys in Australia's history. In his journal, Sturt describes the hardships endured by his men as they made their way up the Murrumbidgee River.

"The men lost the proper and muscular jerk with which they once made the waters foam and the oars bend. Their whole bodies swung with an awkward and laboured motion. Their arms appeared to be nerveless; their faces became haggard, their persons emaciated, their spirits wholly sunk. . . . I became captious and found fault where there was no occasion. . . . No murmur however escaped them nor did a complaint reach me. I frequently heard them in their tent when they thought I had dropped asleep, complaining of severe pains and of great exhaustion. 'I must tell the captain tomorrow,' some of them would say, 'that I can pull no more.' Tomorrow came and they pulled on as if reluctant to yield to circumstances."

Two Expeditions into the Interior of Southern Australia, 1828–31, Vol II, *Charles Sturt (Smith, Elder and Company: London, 1833) pp. 216–217.*

Above: Sturt's men row down the Murrumbidgee River on their journey into Australia's unknown interior.

Below: Sturt and his men camped beside the Murrumbidgee River. An armed soldier guards the encampment against attack by hostile Aborigines.

The Overlanders

Close on the heels of Australia's better-known explorers came the first settlers and sheep farmers. Called overlanders, because they drove their sheep overland in search of better pastures, these men helped to open up and settle vast areas of unpopulated country.

"We determined to start off with all our possessions, viz., two flocks of sheep, a few cattle and horses, and bullock team, well loaded, to a recently-discovered and entirely new country, lying far away, some 200 miles to the north-west, and of which we had heard glowing accounts. It was reported to have rivers and pasturage, with extensive plains covered with salt bush; but we also heard that the blacks were numerous and might give trouble. Nevertheless we started, well equipped, and prepared for a long journey, through a strange and very thinly-populated district, generally following the course of a river running any way near to the direction we were making for, and then crossing belts of water-less and timbered country for thirty or forty miles, until we reached another river or watercourse. . . .

"Eventually we reached the south bank of the Murray river, on the other side of which some 70 miles or so, was our land of promise."

Reminiscences of Australian Early Life by a Pioneer (*A. P. Marsden: London, 1893*) *pp. 54–55.*

Below: an unknown overlander drives his sheep through the Australian bush. The overlanders followed closely on the heels of Australia's early explorers.

The Tory Sails for New Zealand

The *Tory*, carrying William Wakefield and his party to New Zealand, sailed from England in 1839. This account of the embarkation appeared in a London newspaper of May 11, 1839.

"Plymouth, May 9.—Among our last shipping arrivals is the barque *Tory*, from London, bound to New Zealand, which reached the Sound early yesterday morning.... The present voyage is a remarkable one, being the first expedition despatched by the Company, with the view of exploring the country [and establishing] regular British settlements in New Zealand.... The expedition is under the orders of Colonel Wakefield, a very distinguished officer; and the ship is commanded by Mr. Chaffers, R.N., a skilful nautical surveyor, who was master of his majesty's ship *Beagle*, in Captain Fitzroy's surveying expedition in the South Seas. The *Tory* carries a surgeon, another gentleman devoted to medical statistics, a naturalist (Dr. Dieffenbach, of Berlin), a draftsman (Mr. Heaphy), a few young gentlemen as volunteers, and an interpreter, Naiti, a

Above: a family of Scottish emigrants on their arrival in New Zealand. Under the auspices of the New Zealand Company, thousands of settlers flocked to the Nelson and Wellington areas.

Right: a contemporary portrait of Edward Gibbon Wakefield, pioneer and founder of the New Zealand Company.

Right: emigrants aboard a ship bound for New Zealand. These early pioneers risked shipwreck and piracy in order to reach the New Zealand colonies.

New Zealand chieftain, who has resided in England for two years, and has acquired the English language and habits. It is understood that this expedition is a preliminary one, for the purpose of selecting the site of a town, and acquiring correct and scientific information in regard to the country. . . . It is said the Company are fitting out another vessel to follow the *Tory* in a few weeks, and that a large body of emigrants, consisting of most respectable families, will embark from London in the course of the present summer. The wind being now favourable for sea, the *Tory* is to sail from the Sound this evening, or early on Friday morning at latest. The final instructions from the Company in London reached Colonel Wakefield on board the *Tory* yesterday."

Despatch from Col. Wakefield with Journal dated Cloudy Bay, Oct. 10, 1839, *from Supplementary Information Relative to New Zealand, John Ward, Secretary to the New Zealand Company (John W. Parker: London. 1840) p. 68.*

Duties of a Pakeha

"Pakeha" was the name given by the Maoris to a white man who lived among them. The pakeha—often a solitary trader, whaler or escaped convict from Australia—learned the Maori language and acted for his tribe in dealings with European traders. The role of the pakeha was complex and ritualistic. Here, it is described by an anonymous pakeha.

"The fact of my having become his pakeha made our respective relations and duties to each other about as follows—

"Firstly.—At all times, places, and companies, my owner had the right to call me 'his pakeha.'

"Secondly.—He had the general privilege of 'pot-luck' whenever he chose to honour my establishment with a visit: said pot-luck to be tumbled out to him on the ground before the house; he being far too great a man to eat out of plates or dishes, or any degenerate invention of that nature; as, if he did, they would all become tapu and of no use to any one but himself: nor indeed to himself either, as he did not see the use of them.

"Thirdly.—It was well understood that to avoid the unpleasant appearance of paying 'black mail,' and to keep up general kindly relations, my owner should from time to time make me small presents, and that in return I should make him presents of five or six times the value: all this to be done as if arising from mutual love and kindness, and not the slightest allusion to be ever made to the relative value of the gifts on either side. (An important article.)

"Fourthly.—It was to be a *sine qua non* that I must purchase everything the chief or his family had to sell, whether I wanted them or not, and give the highest market price, or rather more. (Another very important article.)

"Fifthly.—The Chief's own particular pipe was never to be allowed to become extinguished for want of the needful supply of tobacco.

"Sixthly.—All desirable jobs of work, and all advantages of all kinds, to be offered first to the family of my *rangatira,* before letting any one else have them; payment for same to be about 25 per cent. more than to any one else, exclusive of a *douceur* to the chief himself, because he did not work."

Old New Zealand, by A Pakeha Maori (*Smith Elder and Company: London, 1863*) *pp. 165–166.*

Above: this portrait of a Maori chief depicts the elaborate facial tatooing common among several Maori tribes.

Right: an early view of a Maori pa, typical of the villages visited by Marsden and other early New Zealand pioneers. The pa was the center of Maori life in times of war and peace.

Left: a tapued Maori chief eats with a fernstalk. As soon as the tapued chief touched the stalk and bowl, they too became tapu and could be used by no one else.

Lake Torrens

Australia's salt lakes, containing little or no water, presented formidable barriers to early explorers. In 1840, Edward Eyre attempted to reach the interior only to find himself blocked by Lake Torrens and Lake Eyre. He describes the seemingly endless expanse of Lake Torrens in his journal.

"The extraordinary deception caused by mirage and refraction, arising from the state of the atmosphere in these regions, makes it almost impossible to believe the evidence of one's own eyesight; but as far as I could judge under these circumstances, it appeared to me that there was water in the bed of the lake at a distance of four or five miles from where I was, and at this point Lake Torrens was about fifteen or twenty miles across, having high land bounding it to the west, seemingly a continuation of the table land at the head of Spencer's Gulf on its western side.

"Foiled in the hope of reaching the water, I stood gazing on the dismal prospect before me with feelings of chagrin and gloom. I can hardly say I felt disappointed, for my expectations in this quarter had never been sanguine; but I could not view unmoved, a scene which from its character and extent, I well knew must exercise a great influence over my future plans and hopes: the vast area of the lake was before me interminable as far as the eye could see to the northward, and the country upon its shore, was desolate and forbidding."

Journals of Expedition of Discoveries into Central Australia and Overland from Adelaide to King George's Sound, 1840, *Edward Eyre* (2 vol. T. & W. Boone: London, 1845) pp. 58–59.

Below: this illustration from Eyre's *Journal* shows Lake Torrens stretching before him. The "salt lake halo," formed by Lake Torrens and Lake Eyre, forced the explorer to abandon his attempt to reach Australia's interior.

Thirst

In their efforts to cross the vast Australian continent, explorers were continually plagued by the unbearable heat and the scarcity of drinking water. Nowhere was this problem more severe than in Western Australia with its miles of desert land. George Grey, an early pioneer, describes the physical and mental effects of going for days in the blistering heat with nothing to drink.

"... not only was my mouth parched, burning and devoid of moisture, but the senses of sight and hearing became much more affected; I could scarcely recognize the voices of the rest; and when uncouth unnatural tones struck my ear, it took me some time to collect my thoughts in order to understand what was said, somewhat in the way one is obliged to act when one is roused suddenly from a deep sleep. In the same manner my sight had become feeble and indistinct; but by far the most distressing sensation was that experienced upon rising up after having rested for a few moments. I then felt the blood rush violently to the head and the feeling produced was as if it were driven by a forcing-pump through all my veins."

Expeditions in Western Australia, 1837–1839, Vol. 2 *George Grey* (*T. & W. Boone: London, 1841*) *p. 78.*

Right: a lone explorer treks across the harsh Australian desert carrying his indispensable supply of water.

An Explorer's Camp

Life in an explorer's camp was often routine and quiet. Each man had his assigned duties which were vital to the welfare of all. In his journals, Ludwig Leichhardt gives a detailed account of how the explorer lived and worked from day to day in the Australian bush.

"As soon as the camp is pitched, and the horses and bullocks unloaded, we have all our allotted duties; to make the fire falls to my share; Brown's duty is to fetch water for the tea; and Mr. Calvert weighs out a pound and a half of flour for a fat cake, which is enjoyed more than any other meal; the large tea-pot being empty, Mr. Calvert weighs out two and a half pounds of dry meat to be stewed for our late dinner; and, during the afternoon, every one follows his own pursuits, such as washing and mending clothes, repairing saddles, pack-saddles; my occupation is to write my log, and lay down my route, or make an excursion in the vicinity of the camp to botanize, etc. or ride out reconnoitering. My companions also write down their remarks, and wander about gathering seeds or looking for curious pebbles. Mr. Gilbert takes his gun to shoot birds. A loud coo-ee again unites us towards the sunset around our table-cloth; and while enjoying our meals, the subject of the day's journey, the past, the present and the future, by turns engage our attention, or furnish matter for conversation and remark, according to the respective humour of the parties."

Journal of an Overland Expedition from Moreton Bay to Port Essington, 1844–45, *Ludwig Leichhardt* (*T. & W. Boone: London, 1847*)

Below: explorers in an Australian bush camp relax after their evening meal.

In the Desert

Above: a horse collapses from thirst and exhaustion. The desert, with its unbearable heat and scarcity of drinking water, took its toll in the lives of both men and animals.

Ernest Giles made four expeditions into the desert lands of southern and western Australia. His writings depict the desolation of the Australian desert and the hazards it contained for Australia's explorers.

"It was impossible to travel through this region at night, even by moonlight; we should have lost our eyes upon the sticks and branches of the direful scrubs if we had attempted it, besides tearing our skin and clothes to pieces also. Starting at earliest dawn, and traversing formidably steep and rolling waves of sand, we at length reached the foot of the mountain we had been striving for, in twenty-three miles, forty-five from Wynbring. I could not help thinking it was the most desolate heap on the face of the earth, having no water or places that could hold it. The elevation of this eminence was over 1,000 feet above the surrounding country, and over 2,000 feet above the sea. The country visible from its summit was still enveloped in dense scrubs in every direction, except on a bearing a few degrees north of east, where some low ridges appeared. I rode my horse Chester many miles over the wretched stony slopes at the foot of this mountain, and tied him up to trees while I walked to its summit, and into gullies and crevices innumberable, but no water rewarded my efforts."

Australia Twice Traversed, Ernest Giles (*Sampson Low, Marston, Searle and Rivington Ltd: London, 1889*) *p. 108.*

Courage and Caution

John M. Stuart was a highly experienced explorer who combined incredible courage with an admirable caution. He lost the race across the Australian continent to Robert Burke, but unlike Burke he accomplished his goal without losing a single member of his expedition. In the process he blazed an important trail from Adelaide to Darwin. His journals show the calm and measured judgment of his leadership.

"Saturday, July 26—Charles's Creek, Chambers's Bay, Van Diemen's Gulf. This day I commence my retreat, and feel perfectly satisfied in my own mind that I have done everything in my power to obtain as extensive a knowledge of the country as the strength of my party will allow me. I could have made the mouth of the river, but perhaps at the expense of losing many of the horses, thus

Above: the Australian explorers were deeply impressed by the size and grandeur of some of the country's natural features. Stuart was the first to see this great stone monolith, and this picture is taken from his *Journal*.

Left: a portrait of John McDouall Stuart planting the British flag on the shores of the Indian Ocean.

Right: Stuart talks with a group of Aborigines at Central Mount Stuart— the heart of the Australian continent.

increasing the difficulties of the return journey. Many of them are so poor and weak from the effects of the worms that they have not been able for some time to carry anything like a load, and I have been compelled to make the horses stand the brunt of the work of the expedition; as yet, not one of them has failed; they have all done their work in excellent style. The sea has been reached which was the great object of the expedition, and a practicable route found through a splendid country from Newcastle Water to it, abounding, for a great part of the way, in running streams well stocked with fish; and this has been accomplished at a season of the year during which we have not had one drop of rain."

Explorations across the Continent of Australia, 1861–62, *J. M. Stuart* (*F. F. Baillier: Melbourne, 1863*) *p. 59.*

The Explorers

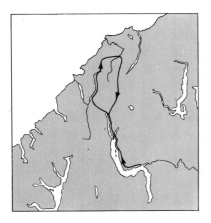

BARRINGTON, A. J.

dates unknown England
1863: Explored large sections of New Zealand's South Island while searching for gold. Traced many of the rivers of Westland and provided many details of the land between the Hollyford and the Haast.

BASS, GEORGE

1771–1803(?) England
1795: With Matthew Flinders took the tiny *Tom Thumb* south from Sydney Cove and up the George's River.
1796: With Flinders explored Port Hacking. Later that year sailed from Sydney in an open boat as far as Western Port, parallel with the western end of Tasmania.
1798: With Flinders, circumnavigated Tasmania.
See map on page 83

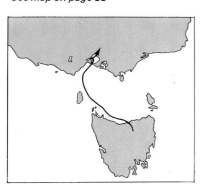

BATMAN, JOHN

1801–1839 England
1835: Explored the Port Phillip district and bought land on the sites of Melbourne and Geelong.
See map bottom of previous column

BAUDIN, NICOLAS

1750(?)–1803 France
1801–1802: Explored the coast of Australia from Port Jackson to Cape Catastrophe. Named and charted the coastal region from Bass Strait to Encounter Bay, where he met Flinders in the *Investigator*. Called Nuytsland, *Terre Napoléon*.
See map on page 83

BLAXLAND, GREGORY

1778–1853 England
1813: Set out from Penrith on the Nepean River to cross the Blue Mountains. Reached the Bathurst Plains before returning to Sydney.
See map on page 96

BOUGAINVILLE, LOUIS ANTOINE DE

1729–1811 France
1768: Sailed westward from the New Hebrides and sighted the Great Barrier Reef off the coast of Queensland. Turned northeast to New Guinea. First Frenchman to sail around the world.

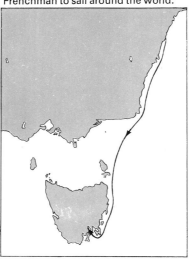

BOWEN, JOHN

1780–1827 England
1803: Was sent by Governor King to establish a settlement on Van Diemen's Land. Explored the Derwent River and founded a settlement at Risdon Cove.
See map bottom of previous column

BRUNNER, THOMAS

1821–1874 England
1846: Accompanied Heaphy in his search for uninhabited land on New Zealand's South Island. Reached as far south as the Arahura River before returning to Nelson.
1846–1847: Traveled from Nelson to Tititira Head in southern Westland, exploring the unknown western coast. Traced the South Island's two major rivers–the Grey and the Buller.
See map on page 118

BURKE, ROBERT O'HARA

1821–1861 Ireland
1860–1861: With William Wills led a party from Melbourne to Menindee on the Darling River. Crossed Cooper's Creek and reached the estuary of the Flinders River. Was the first to cross Australia from south to north, but both he and Wills died on the return trip.
See map on page 124

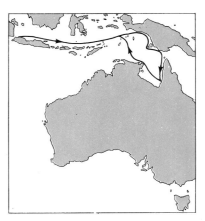

CARSTENSZ, JAN

dates unknown Holland
1623: Sent by the Dutch East India Company to extend the explorations of

Willem Jansz and chart the north coast of Australia.
During the voyage, the Gulf of Carpentaria and Arnhem Land were added to the maps.

COLENSO, WILLIAM
1811–1899   England
1835: Landed at Hick's Bay and went up the Waipa Valley to Whakawhitira.
1841–1842: Crossed the Ruahine Range to Lake Tarawera and continued to Bay of Islands.
1847: Traveled from Hawke Bay to Lake Taupo in the center of New Zealand's North Island. Traversed the Ruahine Range.
See map on page 118

COOK, CAPTAIN JAMES
1728–1779   England
1768–1771: Sailed from England to Tahiti to observe the transit of Venus.
Proceeded to 40°S and then went west to New Zealand. Circumnavigated the North and South Islands establishing Cook Strait before going on to Australia. Explored the eastern coast of Australia from Point Hicks to the Endeavour River. Sailed through the Torres Strait and back to England.
1772–1775: Returned to New Zealand. Crisscrossed the Pacific, effectively removing *Terra Australis Incognita* from the maps.
1776–1779: Returned to the Pacific and New Zealand. Was killed by hostile Polynesians while wintering at Hawaii.
See maps on pages 40 and 118

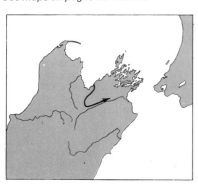

COTTREL, S. J.
dates unknown   England
1842: Crossed the Richmond Mountain Range into the fertile Wairau Valley and traveled down to the sea. Found rich plains for the Nelson settlers.
See map bottom of previous column

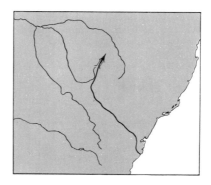

CUNNINGHAM, ALLAN
1791–1839   England
1823: Found Pandora's Pass leading across the Great Dividing Range into the Liverpool Plains.
1827: Discovered vast rolling plains which he called the Darling Downs. Found a way through Cunningham's Gap to the sea at Moreton Bay.

DAMPIER, WILLIAM
1651–1715   England
1688–1691: With a band of privateers, sailed in the Pacific and then touched on the northwest coast of Australia. Landed at Cygnet Bay where he remained for nine weeks. Returned to England via the Cape.
1699–1701: Explored the northwestern Australian coast from Shark Bay to Roebuck Bay and then sailed along the northern coast of New Guinea before returning to England. Shipwrecked off Ascension Island and rescued by a British ship.
See map on page 40

DELFT, MARTIN VAN
dates unknown   Holland
1705: Sent from Timor by the Dutch East India Company to explore the

north coast of New Holland. He sailed along the coast of Arnhem Land.

DIEFFENBACH, ERNST
dates unknown   Germany
1839: Arrived in New Zealand aboard the ship *Tory*. With a British whaler reached the summit of Mount Egmont in the province of Taranaki, one of New Zealand's major peaks.

DOUGLAS, CHARLES
1840–1916   Scotland
A solitary bushman who explored hundreds of major valleys in New Zealand's Westland.
1885: Explored the Arawata River, the Williamson River and named the Andy Glacier.
1891: Explored the Waiatoto River and scaled the lower peak of Mount Ragan.

EVANS, GEORGE
1780–1852   England

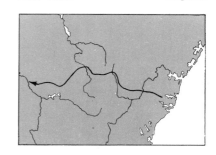

1813: Explored the Bathurst Plains west of the Blue Mountains.
1815: Discovered the Lachlan River.

EYRE, EDWARD JOHN

1815–1901   England
1839: Went north from Adelaide to explore the Flinders Range and saw Lake Torrens.
1840: Went north again from Adelaide in an attempt to penetrate the interior. Was stopped by Lake Torrens and Lake Eyre.
1841: Set out from Fowlers Bay and followed the south coast around the Great Australian Bight to Albany on the southwest coast.
See maps on pages 124 and 158

FLINDERS, MATTHEW

1774–1814   England
1795: With George Bass in the *Tom Thumb* explored the George's River.
1796: With Bass explored Port Hacking.
1798: In his first command, the *Norfolk*, sailed with Bass around Van Diemen's Land, naming the strait after his friend. Explored the Derwent and Tamar rivers in Van Diemen's Land.
1801–1803: Commissioned by the British Admiralty to circumnavigate Australia. Reached the Western Australian coast and thoroughly examined the south coast between King George Sound and Cape Howe. Continued up the east coast, through Torres Strait and into the Gulf of Carpentaria where his ship's need for repair forced him to return to Port Jackson. On his return voyage had to put in to Mauritius for repairs. Spent 6 years in a French jail. Returned to England in 1810.
See maps on pages 40 and 83

FORREST, ALEXANDER

1849–1901   Australia
Accompanied his brother John Forrest on his expeditions.
1879: Led an expedition from the De Grey River in northwestern Australia as far as the Kimberley Mountains and across to the Overland Telegraph line.
See map on page 124

FORREST, SIR JOHN

1847–1918   Australia
1869: Traveled northeast from Perth, past Lake Barlee, as far as Mount Weld.
1870: Went from Perth to the Spencer Gulf, tracing Eyre's route along the Great Australian Bight.
1874: Was the first to cross the Australian desert from west to east. Went out from Geraldton and reached the Peake River on the Overland Telegraph line.
See map on page 124

GILES, ERNEST

1835–1897   England
1872: Traveled west from Charlotte Waters Telegraph Station and explored the area around the Macdonnell Ranges
1873–1874: Again went west searching for a way across the desert. Reached the Gibson Desert which he named for a companion who disappeared there.
1875: Became the first to make the return trip across western Australia. Trekked across the Great Victoria Desert, and explored the Gibson Desert on his return journey.
See map on page 146

GOSSE, WILLIAM C.

1842–1881   England
1873: Traveled from Alice Springs and explored the Macdonnell Ranges. Discovered Ayers Rock.
See map on page 146

GREGORY, SIR AUGUSTUS CHARLES

1819–1905   England
1855: Left point near present-day Darwin and explored the Victoria River in northwestern Australia. Reached the east coast near Rockhampton.
1857: Went through southern Queensland and along the Barcoo River south to Adelaide.
See map on page 124

GREY, SIR GEORGE

1812–1898   England
1837: Set out with Lieutenant Lushington to explore the northwest corner of Australia. Landed at

Brunswick Bay and penetrated the Kimberley Range. Hostile Aborigines forced him to turn back.
1839: Landed at Shark Bay and trekked down the coast to Perth.
See map on page 124

HACKING, HENRY

1750–1831   England
1788: Arrived in New South Wales on board the *Sirius*.
1794: Searched for a way across the Blue Mountains.
1798: Explored southwest of Parramatta with John Wilson.

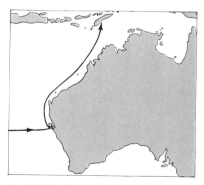

HAMELIN EMMANUEL

dates unknown   France
1801: As captain of the *Naturaliste*, sailed with Baudin to explore the south coast of Australia. Later left Baudin and explored independently from Géographe Bay to the Swan River area.

HARTOG, DIRK

dates unknown   Holland
1616: Sailed too far east on the eastern leg of his voyage to Java and touched on the west coast of Australia. Landed

at Dirk Hartog Island and explored the Shark Bay area.
See map on page 40

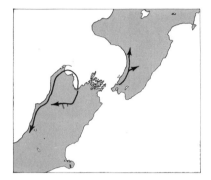

HEAPHY, CHARLES
1820–1881   England
1840: Surveyed the New Zealand coast from Poirirua to Taranaki.
1846: With Thomas Brunner explored the west coast of South Island as far as the Arahura River.
See map on page 118

HOVELL, WILLIAM
1786–1875   England
1824: With Hamilton Hume explored the land between Sydney and the south coast. Crossed the Murrumbidgee and the Murray rivers and reached Geelong.
See map on page 96

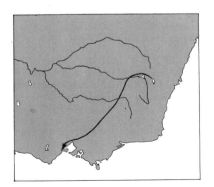

HUME, HAMILTON
1797–1873   Australia
1816: Discovered Lake Bathurst and the Goulburn Plains.
1824: With Hovell explored southern Australia and found a land route between Sydney and the south coast.
1828–1829: With Charles Sturt explored Macquarie and Darling rivers.
See map bottom of previous column and on page 96

JANSZ, WILLEM
1570(?)–(?)   Holland
1605–1606: Sailed in the pinnace Duyfken as far as Cape Keer-weer on the Cape York Peninsula. First authenticated sighting of Australia.
See map on page 40

KENNEDY, EDMUND
1818–1848   England
1845: With Thomas Mitchell explored large areas of Queensland.
1847: Led an expedition down the Victoria River.
1848: Led an expedition to survey the eastern coast of Queensland. Was killed by hostile Aborigines 13 miles from Cape York.
See map on page 124

KETTLE, CHARLES HENRY
1820–1862   England
1842: With Alfred Wills went through the Manawatu Gorge, skirted the eastern slopes of the Tararua Mountains and found thousands of acres of fertile land in the Wairarapa Valley.
1846: Surveyed the Otago Harbour area.

LEE, E. J.
dates unknown   England
1852: Found an easier route from Nelson to Canterbury. Went from the Awatere over Barefell Pass to the Acheron, down to its junction with the Clarence, then on to the Hanmer Plains.

LEICHHARDT, LUDWIG
1813–1848   Germany
1844–1845: Left Moreton Bay, the site of present-day Brisbane, and went northwest to the Burdekin River and around the Gulf of Carpentaria. Reached Port Essington.
1847: Tried to cross from Moreton Bay to Perth. Expedition abandoned.
1848: Started out to cross the continent from east to west and disappeared.
See map on page 124

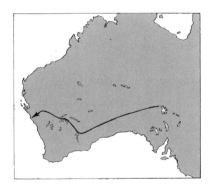

LINDSAY, DAVID
1856–1922   Australia
1891: Traveled diagonally across the south Australian deserts mapping unknown regions.

LUSHINGTON, LIEUTENANT
dates unknown   England
1837: With George Grey explored the northwest corner of Australia. Landed at Brunswick Bay and penetrated the Kimberley Range.

MACINTYRE, DUNCAN
1832–1866   Scotland
1855: Explored the Leichhardt River

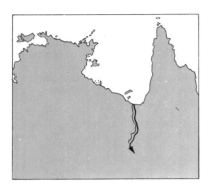

while searching for the remains of Leichhardt's lost expedition.

MACLEY, GEORGE
1809–1891   England
1829–1830: With Charles Sturt went down the Murrumbidgee River and reached the Murray. Found the Darling River flowing into the Murray and then followed the Murray to its mouth at Lake Alexandrina.
See map on page 96

MARSDEN, SAMUEL
1765–1838   England
1814: Established a mission at the Bay of Islands.
1820: Became the first European to cross the Auckland Peninsula. Started at Waitemata Harbour on the east coast, went to Kaipara Harbour and then up the Wairoa River to Whangaroa Harbour near the Bay of Islands.
See map on page 118

MITCHELL, SIR THOMAS LIVINGSTONE
1792–1855   Scotland
1831: Explored the MacIntyre River, a tributary of the Upper Darling.
1835: Explored the Bogan and Darling rivers.
1836: Went down the Lachlan to the Murrumbidgee River and followed it to the Murray. Trekked southward down the Glenelg River as far as Discovery Bay.
See map on page 96

MURRAY, LIEUTENANT JOHN
1775–(?)   England
1802: Discovered and explored Port Phillip Bay–the present site of Melbourne. Named the harbor after Governor Phillip.

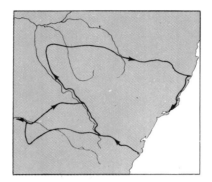

OXLEY, JOHN
1783–1828   England
1817: Led an expedition into the country west of Bathurst and explored the Lachlan River.
1818: Explored part of the Macquarie River and discovered the Liverpool Plains.

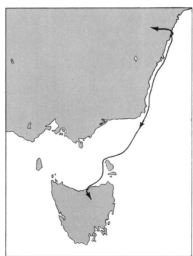

PATERSON, WILLIAM
1755–1810   Scotland

1793: Looked for a way across the Blue Mountains. Explored the Grosse River.
1801: Explored the Hunter River.

QUIROS, PEDRO FERNANDEZ DE
1565–1615   Portugal
1595: Sailed with Mendaña on a Spanish expedition to the Marquesas Islands and on to the Santa Cruz Islands.
1605: Sailed with Torres from Peru and reached the New Hebrides Islands where his crew mutinied and set sail back to the Americas.
See map on page 40

STOKES, CAPTAIN JOHN LORT
1812–1885   England
1839: Sighted the harbor on the northern coast of Australia on which the city of Darwin now stands.
1849–1851: Surveyed much of the New Zealand coast.

STUART, JOHN MCDOUALL
1815–1866   England
1860: Traveled up the Finke River, crossed the Macdonnell Ranges and reached the center of the continent–Central Mount Stuart. Continued to Attack Creek.
1861: Followed a similar route going farther north as far as the Ashburton Range.
1862: Went north from Adelaide and reached the sea by the mouth of the Adelaide River near Darwin.
See maps on pages 124 and 158

STURT, CHARLES
1795–1869   England
1828–1829: With Hume explored the Macquarie and the Darling Rivers.
1829–1830: Explored down the Murrumbidgee River to the Murray. Explored the junction of the Murray and Darling and continued down the Murray to Lake Alexandrina.
1844–1845: Led an expedition from Adelaide into the center of Australia. Followed the Murray and the Darling rivers to Menindee. Reached Milparinka but was stopped by the Simpson Desert.
1845: Went out again following his

earlier route but was stopped by the Stony Desert.
See map on page 96

TASMAN, ABEL JANSZOON
1603–1659   Holland
1642–1643: Sailed from Batavia to Mauritius. He then went east and discovered Van Diemen's Land (Tasmania). Continuing east he sighted the coast of New Zealand.
1644: Sailed along the northern coast of Australia and into the Gulf of Carpentaria as far as the Gascoyne River.
See maps on pages 40 and 118

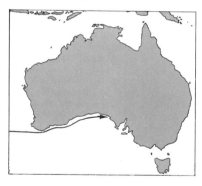

THYSSEN
dates unknown   Holland
1627: In the ship *Gulde Zeepaert* passed Cape Leeuwin and sailed 1,000 miles along the southern coast of Australia. Discovered Nuytsland and was the first to cross the Great Australian Bight.

TORRES, LUIS VAEZ DE
(?)–1613(?)   Spain
1605–1606: Sailed with Quiros as captain of *Los Tres Reyes*. Separated from Quiros at the New Hebrides and continued west where he discovered and sailed through the Torres Strait.
See map on page 40

VLAMINGH, WILLEM DE
Dates unknown   Holland
1696–1697: Discovered Rottnest Island. Crossed to mainland and explored 20 miles up the Swan River. Then sailed north to Dirk Hartog Island.

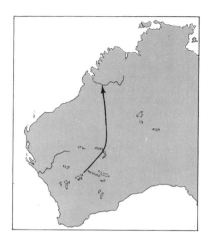

WARBURTON, PETER
1813–1889   England
1873: Led an expedition out from Alice Springs in an attempt to reach the west coast. Severe drought drove him back.
See maps on pages 146 and 158

WELLS, LAWRENCE ALLEN
1860–1938   Australia
1891: Helped explore the land east of the Murchison River, Western Australia.
1896: Explored the country between Cue and the Fitzroy River, in a south-north crossing of the continent.
1897: Explored the region from Tarcoola in South Australia to the Petermann Ranges.
See map on page 146

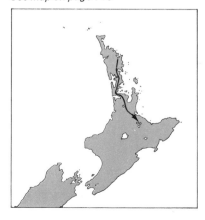

WILLIAMS, HENRY
1782–1867   England
1831: Traveled inland to a Maori pa at Lake Rotorua in the interior of New Zealand's North Island.
See map bottom of previous column and on page 118

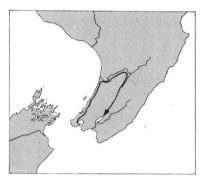

WILLS, ALFRED
dates unknown   England
1842: With Kettle led a party through the Manawatu Gorge to Lake Wairarapa.

WILLS, WILLIAM JOHN
1834–1861   England
1860–1861: With Burke, crossed Australia from south to north. Died on return journey.
See map on page 124

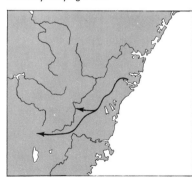

WILSON, JOHN
dates unknown   England
1798: Made two expeditions out of Sydney, across the Blue Mountains. Reached Goulburn to the southwest.

Glossary

abrolhos: A Portuguese word meaning "Open your eyes!" The name was often given by Portuguese navigators to dangerous reefs or rocky areas where a sharp lookout was needed.

antipodes: Name given to places exactly opposite each other on the globe. In the early days of exploration, the antipodeans were thought to be fabulous beings, and sailors were often afraid to venture into the Southern Hemisphere because of them.

archipelago: A Greek word meaning *chief sea*. It is used to designate any broad expanse of water containing islands. It is also used to identify the islands themselves.

boomerang: Curved throwing stick used by the Aborigines for war and hunting. When thrown skillfully the boomerang will return to the user, and it can be a lethal weapon. The word boomerang derives from a New South Wales Aboriginal dialect.

bushmen: The name given to Australian pioneers who lived in the large, unpopulated areas of Australia's interior. The bushman was equivalent to the American backwoodsman, and played a major role in the exploration of the Australian continent.

cannibalism: The practice of eating one's own kind. Ritualistic cannibalism—eating the enemy's flesh after he is killed in battle—was prevalent among the Maoris at the time of European discovery of New Zealand.

chronometer: a portable timepiece or timing device made to measure time very accurately. It is used in determining longitude at sea from the time. The first accurate chronometer was made by John Harrison in England and was very important to the correct charting of newly discovered lands.

collier: A boat used for carrying coal. The collier was a flat-bottomed boat, often squat and unattractive, but well suited to the exploration of an unknown coast. Its flat bottom allowed it to approach close to shore with less danger than an ordinary sailing vessel.

corroboree: An elaborate festival consisting of music, dance, and mime held by the Australian Aborigines, to mark important occasions such as the visit of a neighbouring tribe or a successful hunt.

damper: A round, flat cake made from flour and water and cooked over a campfire. Damper often formed the staple diet of Australian explorers when fresh game and vegetables were scarce.

dingo: Australian wild dog. Dingoes were brought to Australia by the Australoids in prehistoric times. The dogs have proved a menace to sheep and the Australian government has spent large sums on their extermination.

emu: A large Australian bird that cannot fly. The emu weighs about 100 pounds and has long legs which enable it to run about 30 miles an hour. Emus and emu eggs were a source of food for early explorers.

fothering: Intricate procedure used by early sea captains to repair a hole in a ship's bottom. A sail is filled with oakum, wool, rope ends, and dung and is passed under the ship, then pulled tight in the hope that the suction of the water will draw the refuse into the hole as a plug.

free emigration: Australia was first colonized as a prison settlement, but early governors began to encourage free labor to come to the colony. In 1816, all restrictions on free emigration were removed by the British Government. By 1830, approximately 14,000 free emigrants had reached Australia. From 1831 onward, emigration was assisted.

glacier: A slow-moving river of ice. Glaciers are found wherever there is enough snow and cold weather for them to form, and there are magnificent examples in the European Alps and the mountains of northwestern North America. The glaciers in the Southern Alps on New Zealand's South Island are one of the country's greatest tourist attractions.

Great Barrier Reef: The largest coral reef in the world stretching along the eastern coast of Queensland. The reef is about 1,250 miles long and consists of thousands of small islands and underwater coral formations. Many early vessels were shipwrecked on the treacherous reef.

kangaroo: The largest marsupial—an animal that carries its young in its pouch—the kangaroo is a native of Australia and the surrounding islands. It has large, powerful hind legs and short front legs with a thick powerful tail. It moves rapidly by leaping.

Line of Demarcation: An imaginary line dividing the world between Spain and Portugal for purposes of exploration and colonization. The line, originally drawn by Pope Alexander VI, ran from north to south west of the Azores and Cape Verde Islands. Spain could claim land to the west and Portugal land to the east. In the Treaty of Tordesillas the two countries later agreed to move the dividing line farther west. France, England and Holland ignored the line in their voyages of discovery.

Maori Wars: A series of wars which broke out between 1845 and 1870 when some tribes revolted against British rule. Many of the wars were brought about by land disputes between the Maoris and the European settlers. Although the fighting was not constant, the periods of peace were far from tranquil.

nardoo: An aquatic, fern-like herb used as a foodstuff by Aboriginal tribes. Nardoo seeds are hammered into a fine powder and then made into cakes. Nardoo often served as the only source of nourishment to explorers traveling through the wilderness.

New Zealand Company: Privately

owned company formed by E. G. Wakefield in 1839 for the purpose of exploiting the land of New Zealand and encouraging permanent European settlement in the islands.

no-hopers: Name given to Australia's earliest settlers—the convicts who arrived with the British First Fleet. In the first few years of Sydney's settlement, living conditions were so brutal that few expected to survive.

Overland Telegraph Line: Begun in 1871, and opened the next year. The line runs from Adelaide to Darwin in the north and was laid along the route John Stuart blazed across the Australian continent. It was connected to a cable linking it with Britain.

overlanders: Australian sheep-farmers. They were called overlanders because they drove their herds overland, through unknown territories, to better pastures and markets. The overlanders did much to help open the continent to settlement.

pa: Maori name for fortified village. It was usually situated on high protected ground and encircled with trenches. Early discoverers greatly admired the intricate construction of the Maori pa.

pakeha: The Maori word for European. Gradually became used for white men who lived among the Maori people as translators, traders etc. Pakehas were usually sailors, whalers, traders, or escaped convicts from the settlement at Sydney.

rangatira: Name given to Maori noblemen—men who had distinguished themselves in battle and who were important and powerful persons in Maori tribal life.

salt lakes: Salt-water lakes. One of the most famous is the Great Salt Lake in Utah. In Australia salt lakes are common in areas where little rain falls. They are usually dry, as any water they collect during rain quickly evaporates, leaving

a crust of salt and gypsum on the bed of the lake.

scurvy: A disease caused by the lack of vitamin C. During long voyages, without fresh fruits and vegetables, it was a common and sometimes fatal illness among sailors.

spinifex: A kind of grass which grows in the dry, sandy areas of Australia and New Zealand.

tapu: A Maori religious concept. It was used as a type of religious sanction which set something or someone aside, either because it was sacred or unclean. A man or a mountain might be tapu. Grave punishments were attached to the breaking of tapu.

Terra Australis Incognita: Early scientists and geographers speculated about the unknown sections of the world. They insisted on the existence of a continent in the Southern Hemisphere to balance the land masses in the north. They called this imaginary continent *Terra Australis Incognita* and placed it on the maps. A legend of an ideal land grew up, and even after the discovery of Australia, the search went on. After Captain Cook's voyages in the Pacific and after the discovery of Antarctica—the true Southern Continent—the legend of a utopian country finally disappeared.

transit of Venus: Transit means crossing. The transit of Venus was a major astronomical event, which took place on June 3, 1769. It was predicted by Halley and offered the best known chance of calculating the earth's distance from the sun for the next 100 years. Cook made his first great voyage to the Pacific specifically to observe the 1769 eclipse.

transportation: A system of exiling criminals from Britain by removing them to a far-off land. Australia was first colonized as a penal settlement for British convicts. Before 1776, the British government had sent their convicts to the American colonies.

Transportation to Western Australia continued until 1868, but after 1840 it was on the decline.

trepang: A type of sea cucumber which abounds on the shores of the Gulf of Carpentaria. It was gathered by Malay fishermen for sale as a delicacy on the Chinese market.

weka: A fowl native to New Zealand, the weka is similar to the domestic chicken. It was a staple of the Maori diet and became a great favorite among explorers living in the bush.

waddies: Heavy wooden clubs used by the Aborigines as weapons in war and for hunting.

woomerah: A spear-thrower used by the Aborigines which enabled them to hurl their spears great distances with more accuracy.

Index

Picture Credits

Listed below are the sources of all the illustrations in this book. To identify the source of a particular illustration, first find the relevant page on the diagram opposite. The number in black in the appropriate position on that page refers to the credit as listed below.

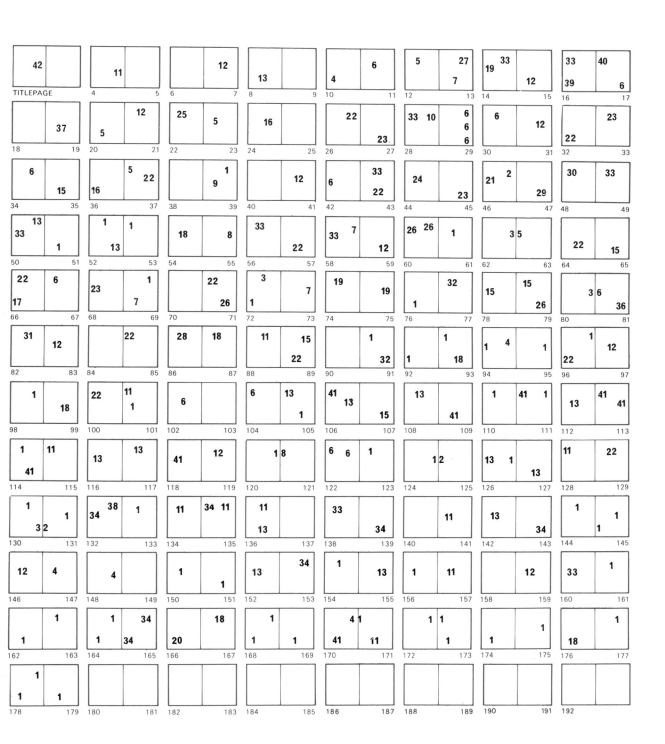